What Keeps Teachers Going?

SONIA NIETO

What Keeps Teachers Going?

SONIA NIETO

TEACHERS
COLLEGE
PRESS

Teachers College, Columbia University
New York and London

Published by Teachers College Press, 1234 Amsterdam Avenue, New York, NY 10027

Copyright © 2003 by Teachers College, Columbia University

Library of Congress Cataloging-in-Publication Data

Nieto, Sonia.
    What keeps teachers going? / Sonia Nieto.
      p. cm.
    Includes bibliographical references and index.
    ISBN 0-8077-4312-7 (cloth : alk. paper) — ISBN 0-8077-4311-9 (pbk. : alk. paper)
    1. Teachers—United States.   2. Teaching.   I. Title.
  LB1775.2 .N55 2003
  371.1—dc21   2002032494

ISBN 0-8077-4311-9 (paper)
ISBN 0-8077-4312-7 (cloth)

Printed on acid-free paper
Manufactured in the United States of America

10   09   08   07   06   05   04   03   8   7   6   5   4   3   2   1

This book is dedicated to
all those teachers who keep going,
in spite of everything

CONTENTS

Acknowledgments   xi

Introduction   1

1. Teaching as Evolution   9
    Lessons Learned Along the Way   10
    The Promise of Multicultural Education   16
    The Sociopolitical Context of Education   18
    Teachers Make a Difference   19

2. Teaching as Autobiography   22
    Remembering What Brought Them to Teaching   24
    Teacher Autobiographies   26
        Sidewalk School—SONIA NIETO   26
        My Journey—JUNIA YEARWOOD   27
        I Teach Who I Am—STEPHEN GORDON   30
        The Power of Connection—CLAUDIA BELL   31
        The Book Chart—ANNE LUNDBERG   32
    Postscript: A Response from the Editor   34

3. Teaching as Love   37
    Effective Teachers of Urban Students   38
    Respecting and Affirming Students' Identities   39
    Care and Respect: Beyond Hugs and Other Displays of Affection 42
    Judith Baker's Tough Problem   43

Educational Reform and Caring   47

    My Persistent Dilemma—CLAUDIA BELL   48

On Teaching Metaphors and Caring   49

    Teaching as Gardening—JUNIA YEARWOOD   50

"A Fundamental Belief" in Students   51

4. Teaching as Hope and Possibility   **53**

The Promise of Public Education   54

    Education Was My Way Out—SONIE FELIX   56

Faith in Their Own Abilities as Teachers   58

Confidence in Colleagues and the Next Generation of Teachers   58

"You Heal, You Help, You Love . . ."   61

5. Teaching as Anger and Desperation   **63**

When Teachers Are Angry   63

Bureaucratic Restructuring   65

    The More Things Change . . . —KAREN GELZINIS   66

The Nature of "The System"   69

    On Homemade Protractors and the Will to Fight
—KAREN GELZINIS   69

Indignity at the Lack of Respect   71

Desperation   72

    Considering Retirement at 26—SONIE FELIX   73

Moving Beyond the Anger   73

Postscript   74

6. Teaching as Intellectual Work   **76**

The Need for Adult Conversations   77

The Call to Write   79

    Understanding Through Writing—STEPHEN GORDON   79

Writing to Improve Curriculum   81

    Puerto Rican Arts in a Social Context—PATTY BODE   82

    Is Teaching Rational?—STEPHEN GORDON   86

    Obsessed by Mindful Teaching—STEPHEN GORDON   88

Sustaining Community in Teaching   90

7. Teaching as Democratic Practice   **91**

The Struggle for Equal Education   92

Racism in Schools and Society   94

Teaching as Educational Justice   96

    Letter to a New Teacher—STEPHEN GORDON   97

Teaching for Democracy   99

    A Way to Live in the World—MARY COWHEY   101

Finding Equilibrium   105

8. Teaching as Shaping Futures   **107**

    The Power of Their Words—JUNIA YEARWOOD   109

    Teachers Change Lives Forever—KAREN GELZINIS   112

Teachers Change Lives Forever   119

**9. Final Thoughts:
What Keeps Teachers Going in Spite of Everything?**   **121**

Lessons from the Work of Teachers   122

Rethinking Professional Development   124

Restructuring Schools   126

Developing New National Priorities for Teaching   128

Notes   **131**

References   **145**

Index   **153**

About the Author   **161**

ACKNOWLEDGMENTS

The idea for this book first emerged as a result of a fellowship I received from the Annenberg Institute for School Reform (AISR) at Brown University in Providence, Rhode Island from 1998 to 2000. Scholars from throughout the country were nominated for the AISR Senior Fellowship in Urban Education and eight were ultimately selected. I was fortunate to be among them. For a number of years, I had been thinking about the central question at the heart of this book, *What keeps teachers going in spite of everything?* The AISR Fellowship gave me the luxury of time and resources to pursue this question. I am grateful to the Annenberg Institute, and particularly to Warren Simmons, the Director of the Institute who took over the reins in 1999, and to the other Fellows, for their vision and support. I have fond memories of AISR Fellows meetings and of the camaraderie in the group. I also benefited greatly from the conversations we had about urban schools and the future of public education.

I decided that the best way to pursue my question would be by working with a group of teachers in urban schools, so I contacted Ceronne Daly. Ceronne had worked at AISR and she was now head of High School Restructuring for the Boston Public Schools. I asked her to help locate a group of veteran teachers with whom I could work for a year exploring this question. Being an insider in the system, she knew many of the high school teachers in the system, and she was well acquainted with experienced teachers who were known as excellent teachers of students of racially, culturally, and linguistically diverse backgrounds. Aside from helping to locate the group of phenomenal teachers who would eventually comprise the Inquiry Group, Ceronne also took care of all the logistics for our meetings, providing what she called "heavy snacks" (huge sandwiches, lots of fresh fruit and cookies, juice, coffee, and other goodies), and finding suitable places for us to meet. In addition, she made the arrangements for our final retreat at an exquisite setting outside Boston. Without her help and support, our work would not have been possible. Jane Skelton, Senior Program Director for English Language Arts of the Boston Public Schools, participated in a number of meetings with us and was also very helpful.

On Christmas Eve of 1999, I was informed that I had been awarded a Bellagio Study Center Residence from the Rockefeller Foundation. The timing could not have been more perfect. In the summer of 2000, just a month after the final meeting of the Inquiry Group, I left for northern Italy to spend a month in one of the most spectacularly beautiful places I have had the good fortune to visit. The stunning surroundings, stimulating company of my fellow residents, and incomparable staff of the Villa Serbelloni all made for an exceptionally productive month in which I was able to do a great deal of work on the manuscript that would later become this book. While there, I was acutely aware of the disparity of my surroundings compared with those of the Boston public school teachers I was writing about, and my admiration for them and the work they do grew even more.

In Bellagio, I especially appreciate that the Rockefeller Foundation invites "life-partners" to accompany the residents. My partner for life, Angel, joined me for most of my stay. For this and for everything else they did to make our stay so memorable, I am grateful to the Rockefeller Foundation, especially Susan Garfield of the New York office, and the Villa Serbelloni staff, particularly Gianna Celli.

I also appreciate the help of Dr. Lori Mestre, a friend and reference librarian at the W. E. B. Du Bois Library at the University of Massachusetts. For years, she has been a constant source of support in helping me locate some hard to find resources and references. Her colleague Leonard Adams also helped me out with a number of queries I had, and I am grateful to him as well. John Raible, my research assistant and long-time friend, helped me get the manuscript in shape by taking care of those many important but tedious details that take time and attention. My editor Brian Ellerbeck has encouraged me enthusiastically throughout this process, from puzzling out ideas with me over dinner with him and his family to making valuable suggestions for revisions. Throughout the writing, my husband, Angel, nurtured me as he always does: he reads everything I write and knows just what to say to challenge my ideas without deflating me.

Finally, and most significant of course, are the teachers. Without them, this book would never have been. First, I want to thank the members of the "What Keeps Teachers Going Inquiry Group": Judith Baker, Claudia Bell, Ceronne Daly, Sonie Felix, Karen Gelzinis, Stephen Gordon, Ambrizeth Lima, and Junia Yearwood. I am indebted to them for their contributions to this book and to all the work we did together. All are included in this book in one way or another. Some of them chose to write, others did not. I have attempted to give a picture of the remarkable insights of them all by including their writings as well as by highlighting some of the many discussions we had at our monthly meetings. I am also indebted to Patty Bode, Mary Cowhey, and Anne Lundberg, teachers who were not in the Inquiry Group but who agreed to have their words included in the book. Their contributions help to demonstrate that it is not only a small group of teachers who feel the way that those in the Inquiry Group felt about commitment, love, and the intellectual excitement of teaching.

I am also grateful to the teachers from English High School who met and talked with me one blustery day in March 2000 about what keeps them going: Darryl Alladice, Juan Figueroa, Karen Gelzinis, Anita Preer, Mattie Shields, Junia Yearwood, and Patrick Tutwiler (Junia's student teacher). Their eloquent words helped reinforce what we were trying to figure out in the Inquiry Group: that teaching is noble but difficult work, that it is worthwhile and essential although underappreciated, and that it is, in the words of Anita Preer, dignified work because "this *is* a life . . . You heal, you help, you love. What's wrong with that?"

INTRODUCTION

"Teachers Are Key to Success." This headline, published in *The New York Daily News* in the summer of 2001, has been typical for news stories about public education in the past several years. The article goes on to proclaim, "A teacher can be the single most influential figure in a child's academic life." In this case, the story was about Intermediate School 111 in Manhattan where several years ago, as students' test scores plummeted, blame was placed squarely on teachers. According to the story, administrators put pressure on teachers to raise scores, going so far as to publicly humiliate them in front of their students. The result? Two-thirds of the teachers abandoned the school within a couple of years. To make matters worse, new teachers, many fresh out of college, were hired in their place. As expected, the situation worsened even further.[1]

Stories such as these have become commonplace because education has become a "hot" topic during the past 2 decades, figuring prominently in both local ballot issues and national presidential elections. Because it is high on the nation's agenda, there is arguably more support today for public education than ever before: a recent large-scale survey among registered voters found a deep-rooted and extensive commitment to make schools better for all children. In the survey, the highest priority among respondents was improving the quality of teachers.[2]

But while the popular imagination is stirred by stories of noble teachers who make a difference, the public is also more critical than ever of teachers. Thus, there is, on the one hand, a curious reverence for the profession of teaching, and on the other, a persistent disapproval of the job that most teachers are doing. What is going on here?

One way to understand this state of affairs is to remember that, although effective teachers can and do make a difference in the lives of students, many of the most highly qualified and gifted teachers do not teach in the schools where their skills are most sorely needed. Urban schools—where the need is greatest—are more often than ever before staffed by inexperienced teachers who know little about their students and who struggle to teach them. In one large-scale study of high schools, for example, researchers found that teachers assigned to low-track classes are often poorly prepared in the subject matter and new to teaching.[3] As a result, dramatic inequalities exist in students' access to qualified teachers, with poor students of color at the bottom of the ladder for receiving services from the most qualified teachers.[4] The "plum" jobs are thought to be in the suburbs or in independent schools. Few teachers seek out urban public schools as their first choice.

Students in urban schools are the ones who suffer most. Weighed down by conditions that middle-class Americans would find intolerable, by and large poor students in cities are also the victims of unsuccessful schools. Raising standards and increasing the use of high-stakes tests have become common solutions to the problem. As a result, teachers are blamed for not reaching the standards that are increasingly demanded in school systems around the nation. Indeed, at times it seems that teachers' work is valued only for its conspicuous conformity to standards-based accountability plans and test performance. While it is true that unqualified teachers are overrepresented in the ranks of urban schools, the sweeping public condemnation of educators has meant that even veteran and highly effective teachers feel the sting of the public's criticism.

That good teaching can overcome difficult handicaps such as poverty or other social ills is by now well known. In fact, there is growing research that good teachers make the *single greatest difference* in promoting or discouraging student achievement.[5] Kati Haycock of the Education Trust has gone so far as to suggest that if we ensured that poor children and children of color had teachers of the same quality as those of other children, half the achievement gap would disappear.[6] Haycock's optimism may be overstated, but it makes sense if we look, as she has, at some of the stunning differences between low- and high-performing schools within the very same urban districts. The students in these schools, and the conditions in which they live, are nearly identical, yet some learn a great deal while others waste precious time doing everything but learn. What accounts for such discrepancies if not good teachers?

Haycock's optimism also seems warranted when we consider testimonies from students about teachers who changed these students' lives. One study found that students who dropped out of school said that the *one* factor that might have prevented them from doing so was an adult in the school who knew them well and cared for them.[7] Or as the researcher Nel Noddings has stated, "[T]he single greatest complaint of students in schools is 'they don't care'."[8] If this is the case, what should we know about effective, caring, committed, persevering teachers, and how can we use this knowledge to support all teachers and in the process support the students who most need them?

Another vexing problem facing schools is that while the number of students of color in U.S. classrooms is increasing dramatically, the number of teachers of color is declining. In 1972, just 22% of students in public schools were considered "minority"; by 1998, it was 37%.[9] The teaching force, by contrast, is nearly 90% White and this percentage has not changed significantly in 40 years. There is little indication that this is changing and scant hope that it will become more diverse in the near future.[10] The growing gap is problematic not just for reasons of equity, but also because there is mounting evidence that a higher number of teachers of color, particularly Black and Hispanic teachers, in a school can promote the achievement of Black and Hispanic students.[11] In fact, one study found that a higher number of teachers of color can improve the achievement of students of *all* backgrounds, challenging the view that affirmative action inexorably leads to losses for the majority group.[12]

These, then, are some of the dilemmas facing public education in our nation today. Given the growing problems and decreased resources in schools, one is left to wonder why some of the best teachers stay in the profession at all.

TEACHING IN TRYING TIMES

Even under the best of circumstances, teaching is a demanding job, and most teachers do not work under the best of circumstances. The enthusiasm and idealism that bring them to teaching dissipate quickly for many. This is not a new problem: As early as 1963, a study reported that the annual net loss of teachers through what was called "teacher dropout" was 8%.[13] A look at recent statistics confirms the continuing high rate of teacher turnover: About 20% of new teachers leave during the *first 3* years of teaching, and the rate has generally increased in the recent past.[14] Even more alarming, the schools most affected by teacher dropout are those that could most benefit from stability in the teaching force: Researchers have found that *nearly half* of all new teachers in urban public schools quit within 5 years.[15] Although almost half of those who leave may eventually make their way back to teaching, the scope of these numbers indicates a major problem in the field.[16] And things are not expected to improve in the near future; projections are that by 2009 about 2 million new teachers will be needed for our public schools.[17]

What has caused the situation of teacher retention to worsen in recent years? No single answer to the question is adequate, but these circumstances can probably be attributed to a constellation of factors: the ever increasing complexity of our society at the dawn of the 21st century, the growing diversity of the student body and relative homogeneity of the teaching force, the lack of respect for teachers, and the relatively low compensation they receive for their labors, among others. But one factor seems certain. The school climate, and whether or not it welcomes and supports new teachers as professionals, appears to be crucial in retaining new teachers. In interviews with first- and second-year teachers, the Project on the Next Generation of Teachers at Harvard University found that the majority received little support from colleagues or administrators in terms of advice or information on curriculum, instruction, or classroom management. Having no access to these things challenged the sense of competence of these novice teachers, and it caused some of them to question their choice of teaching as a career.[18]

It is difficult to reconcile the national rhetoric that education is the nation's major priority with the actual salaries teachers make—teaching remains among the least well compensated of all professions, and teachers' salaries, measured in constant dollars, have barely kept pace with inflation in the past decade.[19] In spite of the relatively low salaries they receive, teachers nationwide spend more than $1 billion a year of their own money on supplies for their classrooms, especially if they teach in poorly financed schools.[20] The sacrifices teachers make are undoubtedly more than those of other professions. However, the prospect of lucrative salaries or posh working conditions is not what initially attracts teachers to the profession, nor is it what keeps them there. The attraction is, according to one study of excellent teachers, "the opportunity to teach well and to know it matters."[21]

Teachers also need to contend with mounting decay and deterioration of all kinds in schools. Especially in economically strapped urban areas, students and teachers alike often experience schools as inflexible and uncaring structures with collapsing infrastructures characterized by inadequate science and technology facilities, peeling paint, broken windows, and bathrooms unfit for human use. They are sometimes harsh places as well, where guards and metal detectors keep the peace and teachers lock their doors to feel safe. Moreover, the dream of integrated, harmonious schools where all students get an equal chance to learn are far from realized: a recent report on resegregation concluded that U.S. public schools are more segregated now than at any time in the past 3 decades, particularly isolating African American and Latino youths by both race/ethnicity and social class.[22]

Dilapidated, segregated, and increasingly staffed by inexperienced teachers who know little about their students—these are the schools of our nation's most vulnerable children, children who also know too well the meaning of disrupted families, homelessness, violence, poor health and nutrition, and other social ills brought on by poverty and hopelessness. The continuing racism faced by so many children is also implicated in these circumstances. Some of these conditions have worsened over the past decades, taking their toll not only on children and their families, but also on the staying power of those who teach them. As one might expect, the result is alienation and marginalization, especially among the youths. Poor urban children have every right to expect more from a public school system that for many generations has proudly proclaimed itself to be "the great equalizer." For many students today, however this is a hollow promise, because raising standards, the means by which most schools are articulating the mantra that "all students can learn," by itself is ineffective unless all students have an equal opportunity to do so.

Yet even under difficult conditions—one might well say *especially* under these conditions—public schools are the best hope for realizing the utopian vision of a democratic society. For the past 2 centuries, our public schools have been expected to be the crucible for democracy. But democracy has not been realized for, or experienced on an equal basis by, all Americans. If democracy is indeed worthwhile, and even attainable, then it is in our public schools that it has the best chance to flourish.

The promise of public education is a seductive hope, one that is hard to suppress. It is precisely because of grim conditions in schools and society that a vigorous commitment to high-quality public education is more than ever necessary. But public schools are in danger of losing their noble purpose today, and this drift in our public consciousness causes me great concern. In the past 2 decades, during which time the schools have undergone a period of constant "reform" and "restructuring," the talk surrounding public education has shifted radically, becoming mean-spirited and antagonistic, with greater attention given to vouchers, "choice," charter schools, and winner-take-all high-stakes tests as the only viable solutions to "the crisis" in public education. Mike Rose has described the discourse about public education as "despairing and dismissive," maintaining that it is "shutting down our civic imagination."[23] The result is a near wholesale abandonment of the public schools, especially those that serve poor children.

But abandoning public education has dire implications both for the children who attend public schools and for our society. I am especially troubled about the future of poor children, who have been the focus of my work ever since I began teaching in a junior high school in Brooklyn in 1966. After all, if schools can no longer serve the children who most need an excellent and equitable public education, how can we claim that education is the best way to alleviate poverty and despair? And what does it mean for our democracy if our public schools fail? Given the current climate in education, I have become convinced that we need to forge a more generous vision of the role of public schools, and we need to do so *now*. Unless we take action on behalf of our public schools, particularly those that serve the most impoverished children in urban areas, we will continue to develop into a nation of haves and have-nots, and we will do so more rapidly and dramatically than ever.

AIM OF THIS BOOK

Over the many years I have worked in classrooms and at the university, I have been unusually fortunate to work with scores of exceptionally talented teachers. Many are joyful about teaching, reveling in the excitement that comes with accomplishing great things. Others are angry at the many injustices that they and their students face, but they take care to avoid the cynicism that comes too quickly to others in teaching. In cities and towns around the country, I have met teachers who struggle against racism and other oppressive attitudes and behaviors manifested in schools, yet who remain hopeful about education as a public endeavor for the common good. These teachers have inspired me; some of the most insightful lessons I have learned about teaching and learning are a result of their work. Through the years, I have joined forces with some of them to investigate hard problems, and we have written about this work. Other times, I have asked teachers to share their thoughts through journals and essays. We have met in the courses I teach and at conferences, or we have worked together in study groups.

One especially powerful project in which I was engaged was the inquiry group called What Keeps Teachers Going in Spite of Everything? that I initiated with a group of teachers in the Boston Pubic Schools. I met with this group of high school teachers for a year to talk about important questions, including why they remain in teaching. In spite of some frustration and apprehension throughout the year, for me the conversations were stirring reminders of the work that teachers do every day, and of the impact they can have when they reflect seriously on that work (see Appendix for more information about the inquiry group).

Working with the inquiry group provided me with some of the most fertile and rewarding experiences I have had as a teacher educator and researcher. Several of the teachers in the group wrote persuasively and, during our meetings, spoke movingly, about teaching. Many of their insights are included in the book. Also included here are journal excerpts, essays, and other writings from several former and current students, also magnificent teachers. The organization and overall design of the book were my doing—and whatever faults these may have are also my responsibility—but the teachers whose words grace it provide the book's soul.[24]

My aim in writing this book is to explore what keeps dedicated teachers in the classroom, particularly the most enthusiastic and unbeaten among them. In other words, what helps good public school teachers persevere, in spite of all the deprivations and challenges? What can we learn from these teachers about what makes for good teaching and learning in our public schools? And what can we say about forging a more hopeful future for public education, one that relies on respect for educators and students, instead of on mistrust and disregard? In the chapters that follow, we provide answers to these questions by considering how it is that superior teachers go about doing their work and solving the everyday challenges of student learning. Each chapter provides a partial answer to what this multifaceted and arduous job we call teaching is all about. There are, needless to say, other answers to this question that we may not have addressed within the pages of this book. But I believe that the thoughts of the superb teachers represented here about what sustains them are well worth heeding.

By focusing on excellent teachers I do not mean to suggest that all the teachers in our schools are as talented and caring as the ones in this book. There are many excellent teachers, to be sure, just as there are some who should not be teaching. Most teachers, however, are decent and hard-working; they enter the profession for the noblest of reasons. But despite their good intentions, many of those who work with culturally and linguistically diverse student populations and with children from working-class and poor families have limited experience in teaching them. These teachers can best learn from others who every day do this work well and with energy and who remain committed to teaching and hopeful about the outcomes. The experiences and lives of excellent teachers can help all of us—teachers, teacher educators, parents, and citizens in general—rethink some of our assumptions about teaching in the most depressed schools and, in effect, about the future of public education.

This book suggests a "counternarrative" to the prevailing wisdom about teachers. In it, our lens is focused on experienced teachers who are especially effective with students of culturally and linguistically diverse backgrounds, that is, students who are among the most marginalized in our public schools. The unfulfilled dreams of these young people—in the worst cases lives of despair—are a stain on us all, whether we are educators, parents, or simply citizens concerned with the future of public education. To improve the situation for the most alienated students, we first need to imagine how their lives might be otherwise, and this leads us inevitably to the immensely vital role that teachers can have.

The notion that "fixing" teachers or "filling" them with new and innovative ideas has become fashionable nowadays as the solution to the problem of underprepared teachers and failing students. In this book, we offer a different approach: Building on teachers' strengths, we advance an alternative vision of what is worth cherishing in public school education.

Chapter 1

TEACHING AS EVOLUTION

A life in teaching is a stitched-together affair, a crazy quilt of odd pieces and scrounged materials, equal parts invention and imposition. To make a life in teaching is largely to find your own way, to follow this or that thread, to work until your fingers ache, your mind feels as if it will unravel, and your eyes give out, and to make mistakes and then rework large pieces.

William Ayers, *To Teach: The Journey of a Teacher*

From that day in 1965 when I first stepped into the fourth-grade classroom where I would start my student teaching, I have experienced the exhilaration, anguish, satisfaction, uncertainty, frustration, and sheer joy that typify teaching. Years later, when I began teaching teachers, I fell in love with the profession all over again. Working with teachers who would in turn prepare young people for the future seemed to me a life worth living. I am as certain today as I was then that this is true.

Yet I also am perplexed about why teachers remain in teaching, why they dedicate their lives to a profession ostensibly honored but generally disrespected by the public in a climate increasingly hostile to public education and fixated on rigid conceptions of "standards" and accountability. There is nothing wrong with standards; on the contrary, it is high time that this concept was used in reference to urban public schools. But, unfortunately, the call for standards too often results in a climate that does little besides vilify teachers and their students. This is a punitive climate that may have ominous repercussions not only for many students but also for talented teachers, those who care most deeply about students.

Experience alone, as John Dewey reminds us, is hollow without reflection. My own evolution as a teacher might not have resulted in any particular insights were it not for the ongoing opportunities I've had to think about my experiences as part of the larger context in which education takes place. In what follows, I share my thinking as a teacher and teacher educator and the lessons I've learned along the way.

I start with my own story because I believe that all teaching is ultimately autobiographical and that it is a process of evolution. It is only through reflection on that evolution that we can understand our motives, aspirations, and even success or failure as teachers. Using my own journey, I want to explore the tension between the *possibilities* of public education and the inherent *limits* placed on education by the context of society and schools.

LESSONS LEARNED ALONG THE WAY

I became a teacher in 1966. But I am not now the same teacher I was in 1966, or in 1975, or 1990. As we all do, I have changed a great deal over the years, and so have my practices and ideas about teaching. These changes did not occur without warning; they have been responses to experiences that I have had as a teacher, teacher educator, mentor, mother, grandmother, scholar, and researcher. I have lately become more introspective about where I began, where I am now, and why and how I have changed along the way.

Teaching Is Hard Work. I studied elementary education in college knowing that I wanted to teach young children. But my first assignment was to Junior High School 278, a troubled school in Ocean Hill/Brownsville in Brooklyn. This was just as the community control and decentralization struggles of the time were beginning. The school to which I was assigned was in the thick of these conflicts. At the first staff meeting, we were told that teacher turnover at the school was nearly 50% a year; that September, I was one of 35 new teachers in a teaching staff totaling about 75.

My first months in the school were not easy. As a 22-year-old novice teacher, I was ill prepared for the rules and regulations that made my work difficult and frustrating: Teachers weren't allowed in classrooms before 7:45 in the morning (there were concerns about our safety); we weren't permitted to stay after 3 p.m. (the janitors needed to leave by that time); we were discouraged from making home visits (you never knew what could happen). I was also unprepared for the cynicism of many teachers, especially those who congregated in the teachers' room. "The kids are animals today" was a frequent complaint. "They're not academically oriented—but they *are* good with their hands," said one teacher. "Their parents don't care about education" was a common remark. Quite a number of teachers were angry, a mean-spirited kind of angry. But teachers weren't the only ones who were angry; the level of anger and dissatisfaction on the part of other staff, as well as community members, parents, and students was enormous. That year and the next, community protests and teacher strikes were the order of the day.

I was young and naive. As the only Puerto Rican staff member in the school, I thought I'd have a fairly easy time of it. I hadn't expected discipline to be so arduous; after all, I had been a student at similar schools. Yet the kids I faced every day seemed angrier and more oppositional than what I remembered. Most of all, I was not prepared for the hopelessness that permeated the school on the part of the students and staff. I often went home and cried.

Becoming a Good Teacher Takes Time. But I didn't give up. I vowed to improve my teaching and to create an affirming climate in my classroom. I worked hard to develop strong and positive relationships with my students and their families. It was a time of tremendous social upheaval, and many progressive books on the crisis of inequality in urban education were being written. I read them all. I was determined to go beyond the canned curriculum I had received, a curriculum so rigid that it included not only the daily objectives and lessons that teachers were to cover, but even the very words they were expected to say. At first comforting for its step-by-step guidance, the curriculum soon tested my patience and thwarted my creativity. I tried experimenting with my own notions about curriculum and teaching. And I avoided going to the teachers' room.

I also sought out teachers who believed in the young people they taught, and I talked with them about my hopes and fears. I remember Mr. Mannheim, a social studies teacher who invited me to sit in on his 8–13 class, a group of eighth graders thought of as "unteachable" by many others. Classes in the school were grouped by purported intelligence. Little was expected of Class 8–13, the bottom of 13 classes in the grade. But as soon as the class started, the kids came alive, sounding for all the world like college-bound students in a well-endowed private school. In that dingy classroom in a dilapidated urban public school in Brooklyn, I witnessed a Socratic dialogue between a teacher and his young African American and Latino students that most people would have deemed unthinkable. What I knew from my own experience—that poverty, race, ethnicity, native language, and other differences account neither for intelligence nor creativity—was powerfully reinforced in that classroom.

In that first year, I started bringing students home with me and taking them to museums, libraries, and other places where they might discover new worlds sometimes just minutes from their homes. I believed that by taking them to the American Museum of Natural History or the Cloisters, to plays and concerts, and to community activities, I could miraculously turn my students' previous academic failure into success. I also started visiting their homes and meeting their families, families who truly cared about the future of their children, and I got to know and appreciate their daily struggles more deeply.

I thought a lot about the power of the curriculum in those first years of teaching. This was before multicultural education had evolved as a field, but even then I knew I had to begin with what was important to my students' daily lives and experiences. So I worked hard at designing curriculum that would help students explore their own world, and also go beyond it. In my teaching, I tried to be tough, demanding, and loving at the same time (I concluded that teachers needed to be, just like a TV commercial about Kleenex tissues at the time, "soft yet strong"). I sometimes worked until late at night. By early the next morning I was back at school, breaking the rules by getting to my classroom before 7:30. I would set up the day's activities—activities that I hoped would engage my students and push them to learn—assisted by a few students who would sneak up to the third floor each morning to help me.

To my great surprise, after a few months of teaching, the assistant principal said I was on my way to becoming a "master teacher." This was, of course, hyperbole, but a great boon to a new teacher who many days went home and wept out of sheer frustration and exhaustion. I knew I had a long way to go, but by that first winter, I began to notice a change: My students were listening and paying more attention, and they appeared to be more engaged in their learning. I felt a renewed sense of purpose, and to my delight, I also gained respect among students, fellow teachers, and administrators.

But in spite of my evolving and more critical philosophy of teaching and learning, being in the midst of the political turmoil swirling around Ocean Hill/Brownsville was draining. There were constant rancorous community meetings and rallies, as well as union threats and walkouts. Relationships between teachers and the community were contentious, and I felt trapped in the middle. I was a neophyte when it came to political movements and I felt overwhelmed by the turmoil. I decided to leave.

Social Justice Is Part of Teaching. Two years after I began teaching in that junior high school in Brooklyn, I found out about an elementary school in the Bronx that was beginning an experimental program in bilingual education, only the second such school in the nation. PS 25, still known today as the Bilingual School, received one of the initial Title VII grants for bilingual education programs in the country. Given what was at the time my rather unique status among my fellow New York City teachers of being bilingual and Puerto Rican, I applied to the school and was hired as a fourth-grade teacher in September 1968. The principal was Hernán LaFontaine, one of the first Puerto Rican principals in the city.

I was enthusiastic but wary about the goals Hernán had for the school. For example, I had many questions about the feasibility of bilingual education (after all, I had never been in a bilingual program and I had done well, hadn't I?) and about the school's almost militant support for parental and family involvement. Within a short time, however, I saw with my own eyes the value of both, and I became one of the staunchest advocates of these innovations. I realized that although I had "made it," most others had not; I was one of the lucky ones. Being a founding member of PS 25 was a tremendous education, one of the best educational experiences I have had. I was forced, albeit gently, to rethink some of my notions about education. After having come face to face with the effects of inequality at JHS 278, I began to think more seriously about what social justice meant for public education.

PS 25 was an exciting place to be at a critical moment in history. It was the height of the post–civil rights movement, a time when the Black Panthers were in the news every day and the Young Lords marched thousands strong in the Puerto Rican Day Parade. It was a time of the anti–Vietnam War movement and of university takeovers. At PS 25 a small but dedicated and mostly youthful group of Latino, European American, and African American educators, all bilingual in Spanish and English, were determined to change the way things were. We were also certain that our Puerto Rican and African American students were capable of learning, and we had the energy, love, and commitment to make it happen. When almost all the city's 900-plus schools closed down for a strike, PS 25 was one of five that remained open. After the custodians' union walked out in support of the teachers, Hernán and a few of the male teachers slept in the school at night to keep the place heated and to open it up in the morning.

The political climate spilled over into the school in other ways as well. For one thing, most of us no longer accepted the notion that complete assimilation was necessary for success. We brought language and culture out of the closet and into the curriculum. We relished our bilingualism and biculturalism and we taught students that understanding the world in different ways was valuable, even glorious. For the first time in my life, at least in the United States, knowing a language other than English and being adept in two cultural settings became an asset. In my second year at the school, I gave birth to my first daughter, Alicia (who, because she was the first baby born to a staff member at the school, was quickly dubbed "the bilingual baby") and I wanted for her what I had not had for myself as a young child: an education that would respect, even admire, her bilingualism and biculturalism and that would expect and demand that she be capable of great things. This is how the political becomes personal, and it was a powerful transformative experience for me.

Because the idea of bilingual education for children who spoke a native language other than English was a novel one in modern U.S. education, virtually no materials were available. Most books and curricula from Spain and Latin America were culturally and linguistically inappropriate, so we fashioned our own books, posters, bulletin boards, and other home-grown materials. Our mimeograph machine was well worn by the end of that first year.

The many fresh ideas bursting onto the education scene after the sedate, conservative 1950s and early 1960s also inspired us. We experimented with such innovations as open classrooms, individualized reading programs, team-teaching, and other approaches. Our curriculum included Puerto Rican and Black history and, among the more daring teachers, an examination of the colonization of Puerto Rico and the history and oppression of Puerto Ricans and other marginalized groups in the United States. We welcomed parents and entire families into our classrooms, and cultural norms such as *respeto*, *dignidad*, and *familia* permeated our teaching. We even had a room reserved for parents and community members, a room often humming with activity as parents engaged in workshops or meetings.

At PS 25, we changed many things: Our teaching practices were more in keeping with new approaches that focused on student engagement; we created our own materials to be more relevant to the lives and experiences of our students; we had high hopes and rigorous expectations for them; and we had close and respectful relationships with parents. But in spite of all these things, many children still were not learning. It was at this point that I began to question many of my assumptions about teaching and learning.

There Is No Level Playing Field. In spite of the excitement and energy that exemplified the Bilingual School, our success was far from complete. Looking back on those first years of teaching, first at JHS 278 and later at PS 25, I like to think that I did in fact influence the lives of some of my students. But after a few years of teaching in devastated urban areas, I realized that something was very wrong. Although I worked hard and tried all sorts of innovative approaches, and in spite of the love and respect my students and I had for one another, too many of my students were still not doing well. This reality was both disheartening and humbling. In spite of hard-won successes with students whom others had given up on, some of the young people I taught continued to experience tremendous failure. No matter how much they or I tried, something was holding us back. It was at this point that I began to question whether the "level playing field" I had always been taught about really existed for all people in the United States.

Looking back now, I realize that when I started teaching I innocently thought that individual teachers could do it all. I was convinced that I could change students' lives through hard work and dedication, and by taking them to the Museum of Natural History and the Cloisters. Not only did I believe that education was the "great equalizer," but I also was certain that individual teachers could turn students' lives around by sheer willpower.

Yet for most of the students I had taught and in spite of my best intentions and efforts, a college education was out of the question and even high school graduation was an unfulfilled dream. Too many of my students still dropped out before reaching high school, many of the girls became mothers at 14 or 15, and most faced a future of poverty and dashed hopes.

Given my own experiences growing up in a struggling, working-class Puerto Rican family in New York City in the 1940s and 1950s, I thought I knew firsthand about inequality. But my work as a teacher with students whose lives were far more difficult than mine had ever been opened my eyes to the impact of daily, unrelenting injustice and hopelessness. I saw that successful student learning was not simply a matter of positive interactions between individual teachers and their students. I began to understand that conditions outside the control of most classroom teachers, including inequality in schools and outside them, prevented many students from learning.

I continued to work hard and to believe that all students were capable of learning, but my natural optimism was giving way to a more sobering awareness of the limits of the influence that individual teachers could have. This realization challenged my beliefs about our society's stated ideals concerning public education, and it changed how I was to work with future teachers in the years to come.

Education Is Politics. "Education is always political" is a statement that the late Paulo Freire made famous in his landmark book, *Pedagogy of the Oppressed*.[1] A few years after he wrote these words, he pointed out even more directly the relationship between education and politics. "This is a great discovery," he wrote, "education is politics!" And he added, "[T]he teacher has to ask, What kind of politics am I doing in the classroom? That is, in favor of whom am I being a teacher?"[2] These words became riveting to me as my own political awareness developed.

Several years after beginning to teach, I was recruited by the Department of Puerto Rican Studies at Brooklyn College to help launch a bilingual education teacher preparation program to be cosponsored by the School of Education. At 29 years old, I was one of the youngest faculty members in the entire college. I was in for some heady years.

My political coming of age took place during my 3 years at Brooklyn College. With the small but growing community of Puerto Rican students, and with other politically active students and faculty from the college, we were engaged in a constant and often bitter struggle to gain support for our fledgling department. Through it all—confrontations, building takeovers, weekly rallies, and even an arrest at which I was labeled one of the "BC 44"—I became enamored of teaching all over again. At the same time, I began to see education as *political work*, just as and perhaps even more political than attending rallies and taking over the president's office. To work with future teachers, and to help them understand teaching as political and ethical work was exhilarating. I threw myself into this new challenge, convinced that this was to be my future. Along with a growing commitment to the work, however, came more changes in my ideas about teaching and the role of teachers, changes that would accelerate when I began my doctoral studies.

THE PROMISE OF MULTICULTURAL EDUCATION

By now, I was certain that I wanted to continue teaching teachers. In order to do so, I needed a doctoral degree. In 1975, after 3 years of my working at Brooklyn College, my family and I left New York and moved to Massachusetts, where I began my doctoral studies. At the time, the School of Education at the University of Massachusetts was well known for its innovative and even radical approaches to teaching. I was not disappointed. My program of studies at the university was thrilling; it provided me with the most stimulating learning I had experienced in my life. But it also shattered the remnants of my dearly held belief that equality and fair play were available to all people in our nation. It was when I started my studies that I began to understand more fully how social and political forces either undermine or advance educational goals. No longer could I view education as simply personal advancement based on individual talents.

When I arrived at the university, my interest was piqued by a course with the title "Foundations of Multicultural Education," first taught in the fall semester of 1975 by Professor Bob Suzuki. I was intrigued: What *was* this thing called multicultural education and what did it have to do with the major goal I envisioned for my doctoral studies, that is, exploring how education could be improved for all children? I decided to take the course to find out.

The course proved to be one of the most engaging I had ever taken, but more important, it put into words many of the ideas I had wanted to express since beginning to teach. I learned that multicultural education, as a natural outgrowth of the civil rights movement, begun by African Americans and their allies, had tremendous potential for changing the life chances of children of all backgrounds. I began to see multicultural education as a humanizing alternative to business as usual, a hopeful framework for confronting the widespread and entrenched inequality in our nation's schools. This is because multicultural education has always challenged traditional ideologies that are based on a bell-curve mentality. Instead, it is based on the assumption that students of all backgrounds and all circumstances are capable of learning and achieving. Hence, multicultural education became an essential part of my philosophy and practice, and it has remained so to this day.

There are many critics of multicultural education. They charge it with all manner of evils, from lowering standards to undermining our children's "ability to read, write, and reason."[3] While some of their criticisms are far-fetched and wildly exaggerated, I share the concerns of some that multicultural education is sometimes little more than lessons in self-esteem, or celebrations of ethnic heroes and quaint customs. I have never considered multicultural education in this way. Such limited views hold an exotic view of culture, relegating it to a nonessential frill, or consider it to be a narrow and prescribed kind of thing that either you have or you don't. Rather, from the beginning, I defined multicultural education as antiracist, basic education that must be firmly related to student learning and that should permeate all areas of schooling. It is for *all* students, encompassing not only race, ethnicity, and language but also gender, social class, sexual orientation, ability, and other differences. Moreover, it needs to be accompanied by a deep commitment to social justice and equal access to resources.

It has been my experience that when they are made better for the students who are most vulnerable, schools become better for everybody. That is why, although I have always included students from the majority culture in my view of multicultural education, in my research and writing I have especially focused on those students whose race, social class, ethnicity, native language, and other differences have resulted in their bearing the lion's share of educational failure. These young people have been victimized not through any fault of their own, but rather because their very identities and circumstances can doom them to receive less than they deserve. When I understood the implications of this situation, I made sure to include the lives and realities of my students in the curriculum; I encouraged them to speak and cherish their native languages; I refused to accept anything but the best work from them; I welcomed their families into the classroom— in short, I did everything I could to let them know that they could claim a rightful place in school and in the world.

But I knew that focusing on multicultural education was not enough. Even before having the language to talk about it, I had been trying to "do" multicultural education in my classroom. At the same time, I realized that a multicultural perspective, as helpful and progressive as it might be, needed to be complemented by a critical understanding of the reality of inequality in our nation's schools.

THE SOCIOPOLITICAL CONTEXT OF EDUCATION

As I continued my doctoral studies, my belief in the ideals of equal education was further challenged when I took a graduate course in the economics department that was taught by Samuel Bowles and Herbert Gintis, in which they used their now classic book, *Schooling in Capitalist America*, at that time still in manuscript form.[4] Bowles and Gintis's thesis—that education is largely influenced by market forces and that educational achievement corresponds fairly neatly with economic privilege—had a profound impact on me, adding to my disillusionment with the ideals of public education that I had so cherished.

The course that Bowles and Gintis taught was one of the most exciting educational experiences I had ever had because we discussed thought-provoking ideas that disrupted taken-for-granted truths. In spite of the excitement, the atmosphere in the class was imbued with despair. By and large the students in the class, mostly economics majors, were cynical about the promise of public education. But the few of us who were graduate students in the School of Education knew that, as teachers, we could not even face a classroom of young people if we didn't conceive of education as a hopeful enterprise. For us, the marriage of *hope* with *critique* was not only possible but also indispensable. So, although I was no longer the Pollyanna I had been when I started teaching, neither was I the skeptic I thought I had become. This is probably because at the same time that I was studying about the limits of educational reform through an economics lens, I was absorbed in the writings of progressive and innovative educators such as Paulo Freire, Maxine Greene, Sylvia Ashton-Warner, Jonathan Kozol, and Herbert Kohl, as well as budding scholars in multicultural education such as James Banks, Geneva Gay, Carlos Cortés, and Carl Grant.[5]

Through my studies, I also saw that with some notable exceptions, U.S. schools have historically reflected societal inequalities quite faithfully. These inequalities, especially those related to students' race, ethnicity, social class, and gender, are mirrored in educational policies and practices such as funding, ability tracking, access to high-status content, depictions of diversity in the curriculum, expectations of students, and disciplinary and counseling practices, among others.[6] This, what I came to call the *sociopolitical context* of education, became a major lens through which I began to understand education, and it was the basis for my book *Affirming Diversity*, first published in 1992.[7]

What do I mean by the sociopolitical context of education? I can best describe it by referring to a letter to teachers written by Paulo Freire. In it, Freire wrote: "It is obvious that the problems associated with education are not just pedagogical problems. They may also be political, ethical, and financial problems." When considering the phenomenon of dropping out of school, Freire explained, "In reality, we do not have children who drop out of school for no reason at all, as if they just decide not to stay. What we have are conditions in schools that either prevent them from coming to school or prevent them from staying in school."[8] This explanation is a graphic example of what I mean by the sociopolitical context of education. Most of us have been trained to think of dropping out, or of failing to learn to read, or of poor learning in general, as simply *personal problems* caused by the shortcomings of *individual* students, or as indications of a particular family's poor habits, laziness, or lack of interest in education. It was a great awakening for me to recognize something that I had in some ways always sensed: These problems do not develop out of the blue, but are at least partly a result of the social, political, and economic context in which schools are rooted.

TEACHERS MAKE A DIFFERENCE

Shortly after starting my work in teacher education, I had begun to doubt that teachers could do very much to improve the situation of the young people they teach. I had, in fact, begun to suspect that the job of teachers was almost impossible, maybe even futile.

But now, after working with practicing teachers and future teachers all these years, my ideas about teachers have come almost full circle. Nevertheless, my faith in the power of teachers is not what it was when I first began teaching. It is now tempered by a deeper understanding of the limits of personal commitment and hard work on the part of individual teachers. While I know that there are certainly limits to what teachers can do, given the sociopolitical context in which they work and the rampant inequalities in educational access, I believe more strongly than ever in the power of teachers. This is because I have seen breathtaking teachers in action, and I have witnessed firsthand what they can achieve. I have also come to understand that teachers are not mere sponges, absorbing the dominant ideologies and expectations floating around in the atmosphere. They are also active agents whose words and deeds change lives and mold futures, for better or worse. Teachers *can* and *do* exert a great deal of power and influence in the lives of their students.

I also understand, perhaps more clearly than ever before, that a simple focus on teaching practices or on technical aspects of curriculum development are inadequate to address the complex problems of education. While vital and necessary, these things are insufficient, especially if we mean to change the outlook for children who are the most poorly served by public schools. Teachers also need to elaborate a more critical approach to education so that they may understand the context in which their work takes place and learn to think strategically about how to change not only the context of their own classroom but also the broader context of teaching.

Given how difficult it is to be a teacher, I've become increasingly interested in why teachers stay in teaching, particularly excellent and caring teachers of students of diverse backgrounds and students challenged by poverty, racism, and injustice. It is clear to me that such teachers are often at the center of student success. Through their daily practice, they play a key role in upholding the ideals of equal and high-quality education that are articulated by our society. I am not so ingenuous as to believe that teachers can fix all the problems of schools single-handedly. On the contrary, my experience over the past 35 years has led me to believe that it is only through a combination of personal, collective, and institutional actions that real change can take place, a subject I addressed extensively in a previous book.[9] This means tackling educational problems not just in the classroom and community, but at the highest policy and ideological levels as well, in other words, becoming active agents for change. But even if they work only in their classrooms—a difficult enough job—teachers *can still* make a difference in their schools and in the lives of their students.

We've all heard stories about "the teacher who made a difference," and most of us even have our own stories to tell. When I address groups at conferences or in schools or universities, I frequently ask members of the audience to raise their hands if a teacher or teachers changed their lives. Invariably, most hands go up. We also see these stories in numerous memoirs and biographies. These are mostly hopeful accounts, and they are too numerous to allow us to dismiss the power of individual teachers. There's the case of a young person who had thought of herself as "dumb" being elevated to "smart" by a simple phrase uttered by a teacher; or of the student who began the road to his future when a teacher told him he was a gifted artist; or of the young woman, stunned when first called a "scientist" by her teacher, deciding that this was not an impossible dream after all.

Recently I wrote the preface for *Narratives*, a journal that invites educators to write about their experiences. This particular issue also included a short piece by Beatriz Campuzano, a high school senior whose father came to the United States from Mexico with less than a third-grade education and who constantly extolled the virtues of education to her. But given her placement in low-level classes and the generally minimal expectations for immigrants at her school, his optimism might not have been enough. In her narrative, Beatriz describes how participating in the Saturday Mathematics Academy at the University of California at Irvine shaped her future goals. She begins the story, however, much earlier in her school career.

Beatriz had been in an ELD (English Language Development) class, while also taking other classes that were too easy for her. One of her teachers in elementary school, a Mr. Wilke, had wanted Beatriz to be placed in more challenging classes in junior high school. He gave her extra homework and made her work hard; he didn't stop until her grades went up and she was able to attend the Saturday Mathematics Academy. She writes:

> In the sixth grade, my English teacher, Mr. Wilke, helped me to understand that I was capable of achieving anything. I began to believe in myself. My self-esteem grew as Mr. Wilke told me day after day that I was a "gift to the world." I loved education because it made me feel smart. Knowing that I had knowledge made me feel invincible.[10]

Beatriz plans to attend a 4-year university, where she wants to study to become a high school math teacher.

Imagine what it might be like to have all the children in our schools hear that they are "a gift to the world." The power of something so simple as this phrase changed Beatriz's outlook on education, and it might do the same for many other children. It is because of the power of stories such as these that I have given a great deal of thought lately to the work that teachers do, the impact they have, their resilience, and the key role they can play in enacting our society's stated commitment to equality and fair play.

Chapter 2

TEACHING AS AUTOBIOGRAPHY

With contributions from Junia Yearwood, Stephen Gordon, Claudia Bell, and Anne Lundberg

Life is each person's singular version of an old story.
Pierre Dominicé, *Learning from Our Lives:*
Using Educational Biographies with Adults

SIGNS IN JUNIA YEARWOOD'S CLASSROOM
- WHY?
- POVERTY IS NOT A DISGRACE BUT IGNORANCE IS
- WHAT IS POPULAR IS NOT ALWAYS RIGHT; WHAT IS RIGHT IS NOT ALWAYS POPULAR
- WORDS FORM A HARD ROCK THAT NEVER ROTS
- TIME LOST CAN NEVER BE REGAINED
- KNOWLEDGE IS POWER
- THERE IS NO RIGHT WAY TO DO A WRONG THING
- HARD WORK CREATES LUCK
- ANGER IS ONE LETTER AWAY FROM DANGER
- WHY NOT?

Posters emblazoned with these and other mottoes are prominently displayed around Junia Yearwood's classroom at English High School in Boston. The signs, a profusion of plants by the window, and students' work prominently displayed on the bulletin boards—all these give the classroom both a no-nonsense feel and a sense of home. Junia's classroom is much like the teacher who works there: direct, tough, warm, loving. Junia was recently recognized for her excellence in teaching by being named "2000 Boston Teacher of the Year."

Junia Yearwood strives to organize her classroom so that it conveys particular messages to her students. She wants it to be most of all a safe place where young people learn, think, and dream. Junia was one of the

participants with whom I worked in an inquiry group of high school teachers in Boston. At one of our meetings, she described herself and her classroom in this way: "I feel I am the protector. My room is their haven. They're
safe here." Junia also wants the environment itself to teach students something about who they are, what they deserve, what they can strive for. At
another meeting she said, "You can't be brain dead when you walk into
my room. You can't [just] sit there. Even if you were trying to tune out the
teacher, your eye is going to hit something and you're going to have to read
it and you're going to have to think about it."

Junia had invited me to visit her classroom, and I arrived on a blustery day in March 2000. She displayed obvious pride in her students and
in her work with them. My first stop in the morning was to her African
American history class. As the students settled in, there was an easygoing
banter between Ms. Yearwood and the 15 or so students in the class. She
sat at a chair like those of her students, but facing them. This, or on her feet
pacing the room, is how she generally conducts class. Her official teacher's
chair and desk, in the rear of the classroom, are often piled high with papers
and with students' coats and other belongings, proof of its infrequent use.

The class began as Patrick Tutwiler, a student teacher from Harvard's
masters of art in teaching (MAT) program, reviewed with students the last
draft of a letter to the editor of the *Boston Herald*. A photo published in the
newspaper a few weeks earlier had angered them. The photo was accompanied by the headline "Root of All Evil," about corruption and crime in
sports. But because it featured a Black athlete in handcuffs, the implication, as students saw it, was that Black men were at the root of all evil.[1]

The students had decided to send a letter to the editor in protest, and
they were working collectively on the final paragraph. Patrick was asking
questions and prodding students to add to the letter. In the background,
Junia was giving her own suggestions. "Maybe we should be asking *for*
something for the future," she advised at one point. She proposed adding
that the editors should be more sensitive, but concurred with the students
when one of them responded that this wasn't really what they were after:
"If they're sensitive," the student explained, "they might say, 'the root of
some evil.'" Another student added, "We don't want an apology; we just
don't want them to make that mistake again," and still another declared,
"'Sorry' doesn't do anything." As Patrick read the final version, students
listened, made a few closing comments, and applauded as he reached the
end. Junia beamed, saying: "Great! I love it! I love it!"

Junia related the process of writing the letter in such a way that it spoke
to the students' heritage (most appeared to be of African ancestry). She told
them that the kind of action they were taking reflects their history, especially the time of the civil rights movement in the United States: "And it

took action. It took brave people. It was people like you responsible for the civil rights movement. They were the driving force." In South Africa, she said, it was the children and young adults who were central to the downfall of apartheid. She compared her students' letter-writing to their budding responsibilities as citizens of Boston: "You have the power in your hands," she said firmly.

The 11th-grade English class at noon was bigger, about 25 students, with African American, Puerto Rican, Dominican, and Asian students, as well as some from the growing population of African students in the community. Junia asked representatives from two groups to do quick oral reports from a group activity the previous day. The assignments were from *I Know Why the Caged Bird Sings*, by Maya Angelou. The task of Group 1 was to explain how literacy was a central value of the author's family, giving examples from the text. Junia pressed the students to link the importance of literacy with their lives today. When one student suggested, "Education was at least one way to gain some aspect of success," Junia answered, "That's why your parents keep pushing you."

Group 2, that day consisting of only two students (a third member of the group was absent) presented examples of racism in Stamps, Arkansas, the town where Maya Angelou grew up. Junia once more probed, asking students to make connections to present-day Boston as she questioned them on racism: "Does it still exist?" The two students in the group maintained that, although Black, they had not experienced racism in Boston. Junia accepted their response and then asked for thoughts from other students. An Asian girl reminded the class of a Black police officer in Rhode Island who was shot a week earlier by a White police officer when the former was mistaken for a criminal. A Latina described racism as low teacher expectations.

REMEMBERING WHAT BROUGHT THEM TO TEACHING

Teachers do not leave their values at the door when they enter their classrooms. On the contrary, as much as they might want to hide or avoid them, their values and beliefs slip in the door with them. In fact, teachers bring their entire autobiographies with them: their experiences, identities, values, beliefs, attitudes, hangups, biases, wishes, dreams, and hopes. It is useless for them to deny this; the most they can do is acknowledge how these may either get in the way of, or enhance, their work with students. Ambrizeth Lima, a bilingual teacher of Cape Verdean students and another member of the Boston inquiry group, was eloquent in challenging the notion that teaching is a neutral activity. At one of our meetings, she said,

"Even in our indifference, we take a position." If this is true, then the best that teachers can hope for is to candidly confront their values to understand how they help or get in the way of their work with students. I began this chapter with the description of Junia Yearwood's classroom because it is in their classrooms that teachers enact their most deeply held values. bell hooks describes the classroom as "a location of possibility."[2] It is also the place where teachers are most fully present.

I have come to believe that being aware of and valuing one's autobiography must be at the heart of teaching because, as the educator Linda Gibson has described it, teaching is "an encounter with the self."[3] In recent years, autobiography has become an ever more popular way to understand teaching.[4] Jerome Bruner, the prominent psychologist, has called autobiography a set of procedures for "life making."[5] It provides a way for teachers to ponder such questions as, What brought me to teaching? How do I see myself in the work I do? What are my blind spots?

The anthropologist Mildred Dickeman was among the first scholars to pay attention to teachers' identities and how they might influence their teaching beliefs and practices.[6] Writing 30 years ago, Dickeman was particularly concerned with the historical amnesia that grips people of European descent, including teachers. As a result, their personal and family backgrounds are either invisible or become another happy version of the Horatio Alger myth. She urged caution in viewing White teachers as homogeneous, what she described as "distressingly uniform in appearance, behaviors, and values." Their backgrounds, which may hide painful histories of assimilation, are more complex than this seeming uniformity might suggest.

Dickeman also described how many teachers avoid questions of difference in order to conform to the cultural mainstream. Coming as they do from diverse ethnic and cultural identities, and primarily from the White lower middle class, many teachers have been compelled to buy into the myth of the "melting pot," to see education as "the great equalizer," and to cherish the notion that being "colorblind" is always a good and noble thing. It is still common to hear teachers say that they "don't see Black or White," that they "see only children," as if those children came to them colorless and cultureless. To admit that there are differences between us has become not just a sign of negativity but almost a shameful act.

Dickeman contends instead that it is only when teachers recognize their own "forgotten, repressed, or ignored" heritages, their own experiences and family histories, that they can begin to understand the students they teach. Although sometimes complicated or fraught with conflict, these histories can also be valuable resources in teaching and learning.

TEACHER AUTOBIOGRAPHIES

A number of years ago, I began to experiment with what I called teacher autobiographies.[7] In my work with teachers, I ask them to write about how their backgrounds or experiences have influenced their decision to pursue a career in teaching. I've also used this strategy in my classes.

I want to make it clear that I'm not talking about self-indulgent exercises in brooding and bellyaching. Rather, I use this strategy so that teachers, while focusing on themselves, learn to focus more directly on their students. That is, developing a teaching autobiography is not simply an undertaking for knowing their own lives more profoundly, although of course it may be that too. It is also a way for teachers to think about how, through a clearer understanding of their lives, they can become more effective with their students. To accomplish these ends, I ask teachers to reach beyond the romantic and surface reasons that people give for their becoming teachers ("I love children" being a prime example). I ask them to think critically about their own lives, about what they thought they would get out of teaching, and about the motivations for their choices.

Many times teachers tell me that this is the first time they've been asked to connect their experiences with their work. After all, many teachers have painstakingly avoided bringing their lives into the classroom, believing it is best not to mix the personal with the professional. Yet when done thoughtfully and honestly, these teacher autobiographies can become not only a revelation but also a source of inspiration and strength for teachers. I've come to see teacher autobiographies as a fruitful way to explore the influence of both personal and group history on the work of teachers. I came to this conclusion based not only on my practice with teachers, but also on my musing about my own teaching autobiography, a short excerpt of which follows:

Sidewalk School

SONIA NIETO

My earliest memories of wanting to teach were when I was about 10 or 11 years old and I had a "sidewalk school" in front of the tenement building in Brooklyn where we lived. Across the street from my building were brownstones that had stoops, so I would set up the little kids (3, 4, 5 years old) on the stoop, and I would be their teacher. I seem to remember having sidewalk chalk, as well as paper and pencils. I felt very powerful because I thought that teachers were the most powerful people in the world.

School was both a painful and an exhilarating experience for me, both empowering and demoralizing. To become a teacher meant, in many ways, to erase myself, to become American (no Spanish, no community, learning to "talk proper," knowing which fork to use). School was the place where you moved from one social class to another.

School was about forging an identity, and becoming a teacher meant losing my identity as a working-class Puerto Rican daughter of immigrants. I brought these tensions and insecurities with me into teaching and I have spent my entire professional life trying to resolve them. At this point (because it is an unfinished journey), I've come to the conclusion that there will always be tension and insecurity, but that it is *not* necessary to lose one identity completely at the expense of another. There must be a better way.

This excerpt comes from one of the first activities that I did with participants in the What Keeps Teachers Going? inquiry group. I had asked the teachers to begin to write their teacher autobiographies at home, but not everyone had had time to do so. I thought it would make sense to begin the meeting by working on our teacher autobiographies for 20 minutes or so. We then read them aloud, at least whatever portion we had written. Mine was quite short; others were longer. But all revealed in some vital way how our backgrounds and experiences had thrust us into teaching. I believe that this excerpt from Junia Yearwood's teaching autobiography explains a great deal about the scene at the beginning of this chapter:

My Journey

JUNIA YEARWOOD

I was born on the Caribbean Island of Trinidad and was raised and nurtured by my paternal grandmother and aunts on the island of Barbados. My environment instilled in me a strong identity as a woman and as a person of African descent. The value of education and the importance of being able to read and write became clear and urgent when I became fully aware of the history of my ancestors. The story of the enslavement of Africans and the horrors they were forced to endure repulsed and angered me, but the aspect of slavery that most intrigued me was the systematic denial of literacy to my ancestors. As a child of 10 or so, I reasoned that if reading and writing were not extremely important, then there would be no need to withhold those skills from the supposed "savage and inferior" African. I concluded that teaching was the most important profession on earth and that the teacher was the Moses of people of African descent. Teachers imparted knowledge and exposed young minds to old and new ideas that were the keys to unlocking the enslaved mind and forging the way out of the wilderness of ignorance and subjugation into positions of equality and leadership.

This revelation made my destiny clear. I had to be a Teacher.

My resolve to someday become a teacher was strengthened by my experiences with teachers who had significant and lasting positive effects on my personal and academic growth. I gradually came to realize that the teachers whose classes I was eager to get to and in whose classes I excelled were the ones who treated and nurtured me as an individual, a special person. They pushed, challenged, and cajoled me to study and perform to my full ability. They believed in me; they identified not only my weaknesses but also my strengths and talents. They encouraged me to think, question, and enter the "conversation" on an equal intellectual footing. They respected my thoughts and opinions and they showed me that they cared. In addition, and just as important, they looked like me. They all shared my ancestry, my culture, and my history. They were my role models.

Upon graduating from high school, I taught for about 3 years at Washington High School. I came to the United States in 1971 and enrolled at Boston State College (which since has merged with UMass Boston) in 1973, and majored in English. In 1978 I was hired by the Boston public schools, where I have remained until the present.

My passion for teaching, my sense of urgency, and my commitment to my students have heightened and are constantly refueled by the daily reminders of the "savage," cruel realities that Jonathan Kozol has written about and the inequalities of educational opportunities and preparation of students of color; the relentless specter of discrimination and racism; the inertia and lack of vision of large segments of the African American community, political leaders, and parents; the lack of motivation and clear sense of purpose of many of my students; the disrespect and low expectations of students on the part of a significant number of my colleagues; and the unpreparedness of my graduating students to meet the challenges of a demanding and competitive world.[8]

The "light in their eyes," that moment when students are fully engaged and excited about learning, that Sonia Nieto has written about energizes, revitalizes, and keeps me focused.[9] I share my students' successes, their challenges, their hopes, and their dreams. My commitment and passion for learning and teaching wax and wane, sparkle and flicker, but stubbornly keep burning like an eternal flame, a flame that I hope burns bright and helps guide my students on their academic and personal journey through life. In the words of Robert Frost, "I am not a teacher; I am an awakener."

In a study that examined what might be described by most people as a traditional, "teacher-centered" educator, George Noblit suggested that it was time to reject terms such as *child-centered* and *teacher-centered* because they oversimplify what are in reality very complex classroom dynamics.[10] Entering Ms. Knight's classroom with a bias against traditional teaching, he left it a year later with great respect for her style and teaching approach and for the underlying philosophy that led to it. He found, for instance, that "caring" in her classroom was not so much about democracy as it was about the "ethical use of power," a new way for him to understand power.

His point is similar to the observation made by Lisa Delpit that African American teachers are frequently viewed as traditional and even backward by some of their White colleagues who may have newer or more "progressive" ideas about teaching.[11] According to Delpit, because African American teachers enter the classroom with a profound understanding of what it means to be denied the right to learn, they often feel a tremendous moral responsibility to teach their students the explicit "culture of power." It is not so much a matter of which approach to use as it is gaining an understanding of the students in the classroom. Reflecting on autobiography and how it may influence one's teaching beliefs and practices can be an valuable way to focus on these things.

Junia Yearwood's classroom is a good example. At the same time that Junia is authoritative and direct, she also wants her students to make their own way. Motivated by an intimate awareness of their lives, she understands that the identity she shares with many of them helps to define her work as a teacher. But she does not want her life to determine theirs. During my visit to her classroom, Junia demonstrated this belief consistently, whether it was working with students on their analysis of Maya Angelou's novel, the letter to the editor, or any other task she assigned. Junia believes, as Maxine Greene has said, that "teaching is a question of trying to empower persons to change their own worlds in the light of their desires and their reflections, not to change it for them."[12]

In one of the first meetings of the inquiry group, someone put forth the powerful idea that good teachers think of their destinies and those of their students as entwined. Junia agreed, but added that others may not see this common destiny:

> Because a lot of the teachers don't believe that. They are not of the racial group that most of our kids are, and not of the social group. They don't leave school and see our kids. They see a completely different world. I leave school and I see my kids. They are a part of me and I am a part of them, period. Most of the teachers in the Boston Public Schools do not share the identity. They don't share that.

Junia's statement should not be taken as a suggestion that only Black teachers can teach Black students, or that all teachers need to live in the same neighborhoods as their students. On another occasion, for instance, Junia had suggested that I interview some of the colleagues she most respected and admired in her school. All excellent teachers, they were of varied racial and ethnic backgrounds—White, Black, and Latino. For Junia Yearwood, a shared identity is significant, but it is just one among other characteristics that can help teachers understand and connect with their students.

Junia's case helps us understand how racial and cultural identity is often the motor that keeps teachers passionate about their work. But these identities are not the only component of autobiography that make their way into teaching. Many teachers also bring their political and sociocultural autobiographies into their classrooms. In my work with many teachers over the years, I've found that a substantial number of excellent teachers are also activists: Many have been active in the civil rights movement, or in desegregation efforts, or antiapartheid struggles, and some continue to be involved in some aspect of human rights work. Steve Gordon is a good example. In his autobiography, Steve, a veteran teacher of 33 years in the Boston public schools, wrote about his political commitment as a significant aspect of his identity, and he described how it had influenced his teaching.

I Teach Who I Am

STEPHEN GORDON

I teach who I am. What I value and believe arises from my personal background and experience—whom I have loved and who has loved me; what has encouraged and hurt me; and the idealistic quests involving myself, other people, and American society. My identity as a teacher was formed through parents, family, friends, successes, and failures. What I decide is true and necessary for my students and me, in both the anxiety-filled nights and clear daylight, comes from my no-longer-negotiable identity, character, and philosophy.

My background helps explain my teaching. My father was a socialist union organizer, and in his household I learned about social and economic injustice and a dream for equality. He had grown up in his father's orthodox Jewish home in the Ukraine, learning from his father the will to knowledge and the precision of language and reason, ultimately using that will and reason to supplant his father's orthodoxy with socialist ideology, which was equally certain about explaining the world. I grew up in my father's Manhattan apartment, finding a part of my identity in this reverence for equality, knowledge, and language. But I also distrusted the certitude of his rational explanations, which could become apologies for inhumane power. I rebelled at his certainty but never questioned its motivating dream of knowledge and justice. I rejected his absolute reason but accepted the magic of language. This explains to me why I chose and continue my work as an English teacher in an urban high school.

Claudia Bell, another inquiry group member, is a bilingual teacher who teaches in Spanish, her second language. About 20 years before, Claudia had come to teaching quite unexpectedly, "by accident," as she said. As a young woman, she had been the secretary for the director of housekeeping at a major hospital and, because she already spoke Spanish, was often called upon to help translate job orders for the Hispanic employees. Many of the workers became her friends and even surrogate mothers. When she witnessed the frustration and sense of vulnerability they experienced because of their lack of English skills, she decided to advocate for English classes during their working hours. Her boss supported the idea, and she became their teacher. It was, she wrote, "extremely gratifying to bear witness to the enthusiasm and pride in which my students used their English to help themselves, each other, and ultimately, the hospital."

Although Claudia had entered teaching quite serendipitously, her childhood experiences influenced the kind of teacher she became. In her teacher autobiography, Claudia wrote about how being in her first play in middle school, *Huckleberry Finn*, had been a transformative experience:

The Power of Connection

CLAUDIA BELL

My experience as a member of that company of young actors resulted in a turning point in my life. As my mother revealed to me in a comment that both shocked and pleased me, "You were unrecognizable in that play! I couldn't believe that the confident girl in the play and my own timid child were the same person."

It was my first real opportunity to feel secure enough to discover my true abilities and strengths, to be respected as a valuable, contributing member of a group, and to believe that I could claim equal ownership in a successful endeavor honestly. It was a powerful experience, one that I gradually learned to replicate in academic ways. I had to unlearn the label previously internalized by me and reinforced by both my family and teachers: that I was "slow" and certainly not as bright or talented as my older sisters and brother.

The image from that play, that connection between support and self-confidence, trust and self-reliance, has sustained me and influenced my relationships with students and my effectiveness as their teacher. . . . After twenty-five years of teaching bilingual high school students, I still believe in the power of touch, of connection, and in the potential resulting from a nurturing relationship with my students. I believe that this is what energizes me, inspires me to work harder to reach them, and gives me hope for their future. My early, painful memories of what it was like when others had low expectations of me are still with me. Therefore, each time I can help a student to reject labels, unlearn failure, and trust herself enough to uncover her gifts and strengths in order to thrive, it is a victory for us both. Her success is my success, and the prospect of continuing is a joyous one.

Not all teachers go through the kind of soul-searching that Junia, Steve, and Claudia demonstrate in these excerpts. But I believe that all educators, if they are to become effective teachers of their students, need to confront tough questions about their identities and motivations; they need to think about why they do things as they do and ask if there might a better way of reaching their students; they need to reflect on how a word, a gesture, or an action might inspire or wound for life. Simply learning "tricks of the trade," or the latest strategy or fad, is not enough to keep teachers engaged and successful in their work.

Anne Lundberg, a graduate student who took a course with me a number of years ago, wrote a piece for that class that powerfully illustrates how particular strategies may have unanticipated consequences. I had asked the students, all doctoral candidates in a seminar on culture and learning, to write to a former teacher. I wanted to explore with them how their autobiographies—both their cultural backgrounds and their experiences as students and teachers—had influenced who they were today as learners, teachers, and individuals. Anne reflected on the "Book Chart" used by Mrs. De Vries, her second-grade teacher. Here is part of what she wrote:

The Book Chart

ANNE LUNDBERG

Dear Mrs. DeVries,
You most likely don't remember me. I was one of the many "quiet and sweet" girls who sat in the rows of desks that filled up our second-grade classroom in rural San Bernardino County in 1957.

Do you remember the Book Chart you displayed? I do. I can see where it was hung in the room over by two tall bookshelves in front of the classroom. It had all our names in alphabetical order by family name: Jiménez, Alessandra; Lundberg, Anne; Medina, Max. It was hard for us to find our names and record our gold star stickers because we never used our last names and because some of us couldn't read yet. I recall Alessandra lightly drawing a little flower next to her name as a self-help device. But this chart wasn't for us. It was for you, wasn't it? I am writing today because of this chart and to share with you some other thoughts about teaching.

I can still recall walking into the classroom on the first day of school. It was all work: boring workbooks mostly, or whole-group lessons. But I entered your room as a reader, so I could escape to my books once my work was done. Maybe you do remember me, not because I stood out, but because I didn't. I was compliant. I was a good little girl. I did what you asked, I learned quickly and easily, and I took care of my own boredom. I had an imagination. Yet I doubt you ever knew this about me.

One day I had to speak to you about a problem. My column for gold stars on your Book Chart was full and I had finished another book. *Mrs. DeVries, where should I put this sticker? There's no more room.* You were aghast. How could it be full? How could I have read so many books? There were, after all, 12 slots! You called me a liar.

You made me stay in from recess and go through the library shelves and pull out all the books I said I had read and then sit next to your desk while you tested me on the contents of the entire dozen. The other children came back from recess and tried to ignore us. I could not look at them. I was so embarrassed.

As you tested me, I could feel the heat of your rage for being defied or duped by this child. You did not apologize. You asked me how it was possible that I had read so many books. I said, *I return one and pick a new one each morning before class starts. I read it when I'm done with my workbook and then finish it up on the 2-hour bus ride home.* You told me to double star the slots and return to my seat.

I am a teacher myself now. I work with young children and their families, and I have been doing this work in cities and rural settings, in classrooms and in natural environments, in and outside the United States, since 1969. And I use charts a lot—to compare and contrast information or to visually record data. But I have never used one to publicly record individual achievement in a competitive way. I wonder why? If I could tell you one thing today, it would be: Take down your Book Chart.

In addition to Anne, several other participants read their letters that evening. Their letters described encounters with teachers, some painful and upsetting, others affirming and uplifting. All the students were veteran teachers, sophisticated in the theory and practice of teaching. Most were on the road to becoming researchers and university teacher educators. For these reasons, I hadn't expected the exercise, which I had designed quite innocently, to be anything more than an interesting way to think about their own teaching.

The intensity of reactions to the act of writing these letters was surprising. We had to stop after four or five people had read their letters and leave the others for the next class. A few cried. In almost every case, the letters seemed to tap into a deep recess of emotion that had until then been hidden from scrutiny. Visible in the letters were both the anguish and the joy that can accompany teaching and learning. In some ways it is odd that Anne became a teacher. At the same time, it is fairly common for individuals who have felt invisible, alienated, forgotten, or harmed in even a small way to become teachers. In part, they may want to erase the scars left on them, unknowingly, by a teacher.

Teachers have so many opportunities to shape students' lives, many more than they might realize. Facing their autobiographies honestly is one way that they can begin to focus on how to fashion more affirming relationships with their students. This is what Anne did, and it is a good reminder to us all that hurtful experiences can have positive results. The same is true of the newspaper article that was the impetus for the letter to the editor described in the scenario that began this chapter.

POSTSCRIPT: A RESPONSE FROM THE EDITOR

About 3 weeks after they sent their "Letter to the Editor," Junia Yearwood's students received a response from the managing editor of the news desk for the *Boston Herald*. It read:

> Dear Class,
>   Your letter complaining about our February 2 sports page was forwarded to me. Thanks for taking the time to write. Whether you agree or disagree with the decisions we make, it's great to get feedback.
>   I read your letter, looked at the page, then read it again. I was studying it because to be honest, I didn't get the same impression from the page presentation that you did.
>   The headline "Root of All Evil" is written for Steve Buckley's column, and the drop head (the small headline—"Money makes the sports world go bad") clearly elaborates the point of his column: that big bucks have ruined pro sports and created an atmosphere which has led to some of the worst excesses.
>   Buckley cites as examples some of the horrible cases that have made the news lately, such as Rae Carruth, Ray Lewis and Kevin Stevens.

Lewis' picture was used because he was the latest pro sports figure charged with a crime.

Overall, we were trying to focus on the big picture—what's going on in sports these days? I know, because I'm the one who assigned sports to do the column. (You could actually have run the same column last week with a picture of the Bruins player who slammed his opponent in the head with his stick).

So, I didn't read race into the lead headline or the overall presentation. And it was absolutely not our intent.

All that said, I see your point.

Here's why: After getting your letter, I walked around the newsroom and simply asked staffers at random what impression they got from a quick glance at the page.

Several said they thought it implied that Ray Lewis was the root of all evil. A couple felt it could mean African Americans in general. But one laid it right on the line, saying we had maligned all African-American males.

You are right about one thing. We do want to attract attention to our photos and our stories and we do want to sell newspapers. If we don't, the paper goes out of business. But we want to be responsible, fair and accurate at the same time.

Your letter made me stop and think how and why you came away with the impression that we were race-baiting. So, you accomplished what you sought in the last paragraph of your note.

It's always wise at a newspaper to slow down and rethink decisions before the presses run, just to make sure we're saying what we want to say.

Thanks again for caring enough to write. I really appreciate that.

Sincerely,
Andrew P. Gulley
Managing Editor/News

When I asked Junia about her students' reaction to the letter, she said they had felt vindicated; they knew it was wrong to use that headline and they wanted someone in charge to admit that. They were satisfied but not overjoyed by the response: They thought the managing editor could have taken more responsibility than he did. But at least, they said, he would think twice before doing something like that in the future.

In the end, though, Junia Yearwood's students learned a valuable lesson, a message she strives to teach them every day: Democracy takes time and hard work. It means becoming involved, speaking out, taking a stand. It would have been easier for them to do nothing. But Junia wanted the students to understand the subject matter of African American history in a concrete way, beyond dates and names and places. She wanted them to know that they were part of history in the making. And she wanted them to know that they don't have to stand idly by in the face of wrong, because ultimately, it is only through the engagement of ordinary citizens that change happens. Junia Yearwood's autobiography created the space in which this learning could happen.

The students' anger at the headline would probably have been forgotten in a day or two, but a lingering sense of injustice might have remained with them for years to come. Long after graduation, when they look back on Ms. Yearwood's class in African American history, they will remember that they wrote a letter to the editor, and that he answered it.

Chapter 3

TEACHING AS LOVE

*With contributions from Ambrizeth Lima,
Judith Baker, Claudia Bell, and Junia Yearwood*

> *To teach in a manner that respects and cares for the souls of our students is
> essential if we are to provide the necessary conditions where learning can
> most deeply and intimately begin.*
>
> bell hooks, *Teaching to Transgress:
> Education as the Practice of Freedom*

In some quarters, it is unfashionable to talk about teaching and love in the same breath. After all, teaching is a *profession*, like medicine or law or engineering, and we rarely hear talk about love as a major motivation in these professions. To be sure, while the word *professional* brings up images of careful preparation and deep knowledge of a discipline, it also implies a certain distance, as if being a professional meant discarding one's emotions.

But teaching is different. Teaching involves trust and respect as well as close, special relationships between students and teachers. It is, simply put, a vocation based on love. In my work with the inquiry group teachers in Boston as well as with hundreds of other teachers in numerous settings over the years, the simplicity of this fact has been reinforced many times over. At our first inquiry group meeting, for instance, Junia Yearwood stated quite plainly, "*They* keep me going," and everyone knew exactly what she meant.

Let's forget the sentimental view of love and think instead about how love becomes visible through teachers' daily work. According to Steve Gordon, preceding everything else in teaching is "the core belief in students" and "a fundamental belief in the lives and minds of students." Sonie Felix, another of the teachers in the group, said her students' words were "constantly swimming around in my head." Love, then, is not simply a sentimental conferring of emotion; it is a blend of confidence, faith, and admiration for students and appreciation for the strengths they bring with them. It is some of these same qualities that make for effective teaching.

EFFECTIVE TEACHERS OF URBAN STUDENTS

Much has been written about the question of effective teaching, yet it some ways good teaching remains more of a mystery than ever. This is because there is no simple or single description of a good teacher. Teachers are more or less successful depending on the context of their work, the students they teach, their own particular personalities and purposes, and other factors. An excellent teacher of high-track students may not do well with students in lower-tracked classes; a teacher who's good with middle-class White children may not do as well with African American students, even if they are also middle class. The question I have been concerned with over the course of my professional life is thus much more specific: What does it mean to be an effective teacher of students of diverse cultural backgrounds in urban schools? Put another way, What are the characteristics of excellent teachers of poor students of color—that is, economically disadvantaged students of culturally and linguistically diverse backgrounds—who attend our nation's most troubled and least supported schools?

This question seems to me one worth pursuing because too many students in urban schools are losing heart and the situation seems to be worsening for many of them. Exploring what it takes to be an effective teacher of these students may ultimately shed light on what it takes to help students reach their potential. In the end, tackling this puzzle may help our nation prepare new and continuing teachers more successfully to meet the challenges of teaching students of diverse backgrounds in urban schools.

In attempting to answer the question of what makes for a successful teacher in urban schools, numerous researchers over the years have found that successful teachers of culturally and linguistically diverse students

- are among the most experienced teachers
- place a high value on students' identities (culture, race, language, gender, and experiences, among others)
- connect learning to students' lives
- have high expectations for all students, even for those whom others may have given up on
- stay committed to students in spite of obstacles that get in the way
- view parents and other community members as partners in education
- create a safe haven for learning

- dare to challenge the bureaucracy of the school and district
- are resilient in the face of difficult situations
- use active learning strategies
- are willing and eager to experiment
- view themselves as lifelong learners
- care about, respect, and love their students[1]

What leaps out from this list is that so few of the professional development activities in which teachers engage (university courses in teacher preparation, in-service workshops, and so forth) focus on these skills or qualities. How, for instance, are prospective teachers taught to hold high, rigorous expectations for all students? Where do they learn to challenge the bureaucracy in schools? How are they taught to create a safe haven for learning? At what point in their teacher education programs do they learn to place a high value on students' identities? When do they learn to be resilient? How many times do they engage in activities to promote close and caring relationships with their students, or with parents and other community members?

Policies concerning teacher recruitment and retention are also disturbingly at odds with promoting the qualities that teachers need to develop to be successful with students of diverse backgrounds. For instance, rather than being encouraged through various incentives to remain in urban schools, the most experienced teachers are rewarded when they *leave* urban schools for wealthier suburban schools. The disconnect between the needs of students in urban schools and the policies for retaining the best teachers in the schools that most need them is nothing short of staggering.

In this chapter, I'd like to pursue more closely two particular aspects of love embedded in effective teaching: *respecting and affirming students' identities*; and *demonstrating care and respect* for students.

RESPECTING AND AFFIRMING STUDENTS' IDENTITIES

In my work with teachers, I've found that the most caring and compassionate among them subscribe to a common philosophy: They believe that supporting and affirming students' identities *while at the same time* encouraging students to become members of the larger community when they are ready and able is in the long run a better way to help students adjust to school and, ultimately, to life beyond school. This is one tangible way in which they demonstrate the love they have for their students. A case in point is that of Ambrizeth Lima, a former high school bilingual teacher of Cape Verdean students and herself an immigrant from the Cape Verde

Islands. A participant in the inquiry group, Ambrizeth wrote about her immigrant experience and how it had helped her understand her students better:

> I believe that what has inspired me throughout my academic and teaching career are the strong ties I have to my community and my heritage. The fact that I arrived in this country at a stage in my life when I understood who I was and embraced my culture and my race gave me strength to continue my education, in spite of the odds.
>
> My students, many times, are urged to forget who they are, or told that they must "become American," as if they could. The message that they get many times is that they must discard themselves of their own racial, ethnic, or linguistic identity. In their attempt to assimilate, many of them lose themselves. They get frustrated because no matter how much they try, they will never be accepted as "American." Others, because they resent the message that they must shed every facet of their own identity, resist the pressure and alienate themselves. These students usually drop out of school, get in trouble with the law, and are put in jail or deported. It seems that those who become bicultural have a strong sense of identity that adds balance in their lives; at least this is my hypothesis.

Ambrizeth's approach to teaching immigrant students is also reflected in the growing literature about the link between identity and learning. As she so eloquently expressed it, far too many students believe that they must "discard themselves" of their identity in order to fit in. In my own research with a number of academically successful secondary school students of various backgrounds, I found that although these young people wanted to connect with their peers, and they were sometimes embarrassed by their immigrant or nonmainstream backgrounds, they were also fiercely committed to maintaining a connection with their native languages and ethnic/racial cultures.[2] In reviewing research on the adaptation and assimilation among immigrant students, Alejandro Portes and Rubén Rumbaut came to a similar conclusion: They found that young people of immigrant backgrounds who undergo what the researchers call a "premature assimilation" are more at risk for academic failure and emotional distress than are young people whose assimilation is more gradual.[3]

The effect that affirming students' identities can have on learning has been the subject of much educational research in the past decade or so.[4] In summarizing studies that looked at the influence of identity on immigrant students in U.S. schools, for instance, Margaret Gibson concluded that students whose ethnicity is valued are more likely to connect strongly and positively with school and learning. This finding squarely contradicts a central role that schools are expected to play—to be a crucible, a place where differences are erased so that the playing field is leveled. But Gibson, among many other researchers, has found just the opposite to be the case. Her conclusion is no less dramatic. "In other words," she writes, "the best course for second-generation immigrant youth appears to be one that encourages them to remain securely anchored in their ethnic communities while pursuing a strategy of paced, selective acculturation."[5] But this is true not only for immigrant students; it seems to hold true for others as well. For instance, a consistent finding concerning African American students is that when their teachers understand, appreciate, and use these students' culture in the service of their education, the students are better able to reach high levels of achievement.[6]

What does this mean for teachers and schools? In spite of the importance of the topic of identity for many students, particularly students who never see their lives reflected in the school curriculum, making space for discussions of identity is not a priority in most classrooms. Even in schools where teachers are committed and work hard to design learning environments that are equitable for all students, ignorance about race and ethnicity prevail among many teachers. This is particularly true for teachers of European American backgrounds. Ignorance about social class, language, and other differences is likewise common among teachers because their experience with diversity of all kinds may be limited. When issues of difference become too demanding, too conflict ridden, and too contentious to address, they remain hidden.

The lack of will to address differences is above all true of race and racism, a topic that only recently has been let out of the box and aired. White teachers, according to Julie Kailin, operate from what she calls an "impaired consciousness" about race and racism.[7] In research that she did in a "liberal" school, she found that most teachers, even when they witnessed colleagues' racist behaviors, were quick to dismiss or ignore it. Kailin describes the discourse of White teachers as the language of "liberal denial." Her findings, sadly, are not unique.[8]

Yet students' identities do not disappear simply because schools refuse to face them. Their identities, especially in the case of young adolescents of middle and high school age, loom large. Young people of this age always are questioning who they are, where they belong, and how they fit in. When the adults in a school refuse to speak about these topics, or to include them even peripherally in the curriculum, students get the feeling that they must "lose themselves," in the words of Ambrizeth Lima, if they are to succeed.

It is not only teachers of color, however, who can forge deep connections with students of diverse backgrounds. Karen Gelzinis, for instance, at a meeting I had with a number of teachers, was bursting with pride at the accomplishments of Juan Figueroa, a young teacher in her school:

> You know, what keeps me going is that I see in one generation, here's Juan graduated from B.C. [Boston College] High, went to Latin School . . . . These kids were *me*. You know, I grew up in the city too, and that's what keeps me going. All the other stuff you had was crazy, but it's when you make that one-to-one connection with a kid and a kid finally says, "Now I get it!" that just makes everything else seem just so right.

In spite of the fact that Karen's ethnic background and school experiences were so different from Juan's, her assertion that "these kids were *me*" is testimony to the capacity of teachers to connect with young people in spite of these differences and to celebrate their successes.

CARE AND RESPECT: BEYOND HUGS AND OTHER DISPLAYS OF AFFECTION

What does it mean to "care," particularly with respect to teaching and learning? Recent attention has focused on the issue of care and on its central but often underappreciated role in schools.[9] For students whose cultural and language backgrounds differ from the mainstream, care is especially relevant because when students feel their teachers care about them, they also feel they belong. Without a feeling of belonging, learning can suffer. There is evidence, for instance, that African American students who believe that their teachers care about them are more academically successful than those who do not perceive this to be the case.[10] This kind of care is not to be confused with the sentimental variety that is depicted in most movies about teaching. No, care means much more than this.

Often misunderstood as simple displays of affection (a pat on the back, sometimes a hug for younger children), care is much more. It is not just a show of benevolence or a gift to "the needy," but a solid faith in the capability of students to learn, sometimes in spite of evidence to the contrary. This is certainly true among the most effective teachers I've seen in urban schools who, against all the odds, believe in their students.

High expectations need to be based not just on IQ scores or even on past achievements, but on an unshakeable belief that, with hard work and support, all students are capable of reaching tremendous heights. Judith Baker, a participant in the inquiry group, brought in the problem of poor achievement among her African American and Latino male students. While trying to puzzle out the causes of this problem, she was quick to declare that these young people were both smart and capable. She asserted forcibly "I *know* that the boys can do it!" This is the kind of faith to which I am referring. When students perceive that their teachers believe in their ability, students begin to think about achievement as related to effort, not just to innate talent. The importance of this attitude is attested to by Janine Bempechat, who, reviewing the research concerning African American and Latino students who succeed in school, reported that in general those who attribute their success to hard work and effort rather than to innate intelligence tend to do better in school.[11] That is, young people who perceive intelligence as unfixed and changeable are more likely to tackle difficult tasks and to rebound from failure.

JUDITH BAKER'S TOUGH PROBLEM

Judith Baker is a veteran teacher, having spent more than 20 years teaching first social studies and then English in the Boston public schools. Her political activism in the community complements the work she does with her students. Judith had not originally intended to become a teacher, but a growing dissatisfaction with economics, the field she majored in at Harvard University, led her to consider teaching. Her reputation as an excellent teacher of urban students was the catalyst for a doctoral dissertation that focused on her and her classroom. In an interview for the study, Judith had said, "The first day I taught I was hooked."[12]

Judith agreed to be the first one in the inquiry group to bring in a "tough problem" for the rest of us to consider. This is how she presented the problem with "Danny":

> I have this student who, at the beginning of the year, it was almost like he was hateful towards people. I know he wasn't hateful; he was just so nasty and he swore all the time and he wouldn't do the work, and he was failing and disruptive and just ridiculous. I thought, "He must be 17." You know how they get.
>
> So I sat down with him and I said, "Come on, you've got to tell me what's going on here." So I took a piece of paper and I said, "Tell me how you feel." So first of all [he said], "I'm feeling lazy. I don't feel like doing this work." So I wrote down "lazy." Then he said, "Plus, it's boring. I'm not interested by it. . . ."
>
> So I wrote all this stuff down that he said. I said, "What if *these* [pointing to the words she had written down] aren't the real you?

What if this isn't really you? Where could these things have come from? What if this was something somebody did to you? You weren't born that way, right? It's not genetic. And it's not like in your race, your ethnicity, or your nationality? It's not like that, right?" "No, no, no," [he said]. "Are you really like this?" He said "No." I said, "Well, tell me what you'd like to accomplish in your life." Well, you know, he wanted to be really smart, he wanted to be rich, he'd like to be this and that. . . . You can imagine, normal things.

So then I drew these lines [separating how the student had described himself and what he wanted to accomplish in life] and I said "Well, obviously, if one thought there was a link between education and these things over here, then there's a wall there. So, let's try to figure out how the wall got there."

I'm very, very worried about the boys. He was one of the boys in my school and he decided that in fact these [attitudes] were really obstacles. These were really hurting him. He decided that maybe they weren't in his personality, that maybe what he experienced as laziness or what he experienced as boredom with material had other reasons and maybe he could figure those things out. Maybe we could work together to figure those things out. Maybe we could somehow figure it out in school.

This is not like a drama or anything, [but] he had a B in my class at the end of the term. He was like an F and all of a sudden he came in like 2 weeks later and brings in this notebook full of work. Full of just work, work, work. And we had had a conference about this boy with all of his teachers and his teachers were terrified that they were going to kick him out of school.

When she had finished telling the story, Judith came back to the problem she had partially described with this young man, the problem of young African American males who are intelligent but disengaged in school. She did this by bringing in examples of work of a number of students, and she continued:

I want to show you some things that I've been collecting. I've taken their names off. These are the grade sheets for all the kids in this class. Let's spend a couple of minutes looking at the grade sheets and see if there's a difference. And I brought some essays and I brought some notebooks.

I was hoping to take just 5 minutes and look at boys' work and look at girls' work—and sometimes you won't know and that's good—just to see if you can help me notice. I know that not every girl is an

A and I know that it's not easy to make [these] characterizations but see what you notice. So, after you read a couple of pages, then pass or look at somebody else's. And then there's a whole bunch of tests. So, you can look at those too. Take a couple of grade sheets, a couple of essays, one notebook maybe. These are mostly boys' notebooks, a couple of girls', but mostly boys. This is essentially all of the work of the term. So it's almost all A's for the girls and D's for the boys, period after period. We don't have to spend a whole lot of time, just to give you a little bit of work and hear the kids themselves. I'm sure you hear your own kids, so it's not that different, but look at this information and see what in the world I can figure out.

Right after presenting the students' work, Judith added, "Each segment of the news the last few nights, it's been like, 'What's happening to the boys of America?' They were talking about the suicide rate, the [low] number of kids going to college . . ."

Sonie then noted that something similar had taken place between her and a number of young African American men in her classes the previous year. She had decided to do some research about this same problem, she said, because "I was wondering, what am I doing wrong? What's going on?" Her students' grades had also been very poor so she "took the time and I asked them the same type of questions that you asked." She continued,

And I found that there *is* a difference in their scores the next term because (I know that everyone says this; we've read this for a long time, you probably know better than I do) I'm making a *personal connection*. Maybe it was the conversation that you had with him that [made the difference].

Judith stated that the issue of "personal connection" didn't fully explain to her the change in the young man, and she maintained that what she was looking for wasn't really suggestions or explanations, but to have us help her "notice more." The conversation went on for a long time, with people offering different suggestions or asking more questions. Junia offered the following thought:

I'm wondering if with some of them, they really could do better and they're just ashamed to do better because they'll be on the outs with their peers and with some others, and that they don't feel quite worthy. You know, you lose your identity. When you identify as a student, then you lose your identity as whatever you are, and that's something I think a lot of the kids face.

Before we disbanded for the day, somebody asked Judith how she knew that the boys were in fact more capable than they let on, and she answered:

> From class discussion. That is, the same kid that is getting an F and is really giving you nothing in writing is solving the trickiest and most subtle [problems] in class. So I know, I *absolutely know* that in terms of logic and comprehension, this kid is actually more capable of work than this young lady, who has 50 pages of notes—and all of those notes are the most simplistic. . . . There's no reasoning whatsoever [in the notes], just hard work. It's going to pay off for her; she's going to get to the more complex [understanding] because she's doing all this hard work. But I *know* that the boys can do it, and once in a while, I can see it because they'll do something.
>
> I'm sure that these guys can do far better than they are, *absolutely*, *positively*. I really do think so and I get to see it once in a while and I'm trying to find a way because I know if they don't do it very often, they're not going to get better. They're going to be very stagnant in their skills.

At a meeting several months later, Judith returned once again to the problem with Danny, and she described how he had started becoming more deeply aware of the consequences of his behavior and attitudes:

> In fact, he has another set of ideas that are sort of submerged. He really wishes that he was as smart as anyone else walking around and he could read and write and do things. That's what he *really* wishes. Well, he certainly didn't project that to me. I mean, not in the group. You know, he said [to me], "You think I've been brainwashed, don't you?" I said, "Well, who would do that to you?" He says, "Well, I suppose they want Black people to think that they're stupid, huh?" I mean, this is not *me* saying something. I said, "Danny, where did you get this idea? I don't believe that you came in here, read something, and made a decision that this [behavior] is pointless."
>
> It hasn't transformed him as a student to the point where he's the A student or anything. [But] he's never been uncooperative since that day. Never once.

I wish I could tell you that these conversations led to discovering the "right" approach Judith could use to work with the young men she was so worried about. It didn't.

I include this rather long excerpt to make the point that teachers' discussions are not always easy. They rarely result in a speedy solution to persistent problems, and they often raise more questions than they answer. But they give us a glimpse into teachers' thinking about the students they love and they demonstrate how such dialogue both stimulates creative ideas and cements closer ties with peers.

EDUCATIONAL REFORM AND CARING

If meaningful change is to happen, however, it cannot remain at the level of individual teachers only. It needs to also happen at the level of entire schools and school districts. That is, change needs to affect the climate of the school as manifested through its policies, practices, and structures. The reform era that began in the late 1980s, for instance, signaled "care" as an important element of change leading to the kinds of relationships that must be nurtured in schools.[13]

The links that exist between school reform and caring are sometimes striking. In a discussion of the changes that resulted from reform efforts in four urban high schools, Nancie Zane found that discipline problems, which had previously figured prominently in teachers' conversations, receded to the background. Structural changes in the schools included more democratic decision-making mechanisms for teachers and students and a greater focus on relationships. As a result of these changes, teachers developed higher expectations for students, and students' behavior improved as they began to feel more competent. In effect, because the nature of the school environment had changed, the context in which learning took place changed as well. As one student described it, "It's not cool to be dumb here."[14] This is caring at its best.

Conversely, when the school climate even inadvertently gives students disaffirming and negative messages, teachers' best attempts to demonstrate caring may fail. In a study of Latino immigrant youths and their teachers, Susan Katz found that Latino students named their teachers' discrimination against them as the primary cause of their disengagement from school. Meanwhile, the teachers felt that they were doing the very best they could for the students. Katz's research explores how teachers' attitudes and practices, although perceived by students as racist, were probably a result of structural conditions in the school (such as tracking and high teacher turnover) that precluded caring relationships.[15]

Nevertheless, although the research in these two studies draws attention to school- and districtwide efforts that can lead to a greater focus on caring, teachers and students cannot always afford to wait for whole schools to make the needed changes. Sometimes teachers can prod the system. Claudia Bell, another teacher in the inquiry group, engaged in research that provides a compelling example of how teachers' attitudes and practices can also influence student learning. Claudia's research question in the group was based on a problem she was noticing in her students. She wrote in part:

My Persistent Dilemma

CLAUDIA BELL

My persistent personal dilemma is how to energize and encourage unmotivated, discouraged students to interrupt their cycle of continuous academic failure and develop better strategies and a sense of optimism that can lead to their academic success. As an example, I have a group of 17 Hispanic students (3 males, 14 females) in my health class. Three-quarters of them have a history of failure and are presently failing most or all of their academic subjects, including mine. I would like the inquiry group to join me in exploring a range of possible factors that might influence and contribute to their lack of motivation and pessimistic attitude.

Upon further investigation, Claudia discovered that most of her students were failing *all* their classes, including hers. In her 25 years of teaching, this had never before happened. She decided to talk with her students about what was happening at home and at school that might be leading to this situation. With input from Junia Yearwood and Karen Gelzinis, two inquiry group teachers who worked at the same high school, she developed a questionnaire and interviewed 14 of the students. She also gave them individual journals to keep for themselves, and some of them had shared their journals with her, journals that she said were "amazing."

Claudia was taken aback by some of the students' answers to her questions. For example, although she thought of most of them as competent and capable, most of them described themselves as "just average." The saddest thing, she said, was that most of them could not think of *any* strengths they had. But what was most interesting, Claudia said, was that the very process of interviewing the students brought her closer to them. She mused,

> I always thought I had a really close relationship with them. But somehow, through this process, they opened up to me in ways that I didn't expect. . . . I had to listen to some sad, disturbing things. I ended up having to give them all my home phone number because really, there just wasn't enough time to really deal with all these issues! I mean you can't tell them they can't unload all these things; it doesn't work that way. . . . I mean, there's some heavy-duty things going on.

Nobody was more surprised than Claudia at what happened next. In the process of interviewing them, speaking to them when they called her at home, and reading the journals they shared with her, she noticed that within weeks her students were doing their homework much more consistently, and their schoolwork in general had improved. Claudia didn't see this as a miracle cure for low achievement. In fact, it initially bothered her that they were probably doing these things mostly to please her, rather than for themselves. But as a result of this preliminary exploration, she connected several of the students with school-based counselors as well as with community-based resource people who could provide the kind of professional help from which they could benefit.

The powerful lesson to be learned from Claudia Bell's case was that her students' behavior changed dramatically as a result of a change in the relationship they had with her. Although she had always thought of this relationship as being close, it was only when she asked them questions about their lives, only when they began to feel accepted for who they were—in spite of the many difficult situations they described to her—and only when they became complete human beings in the classroom that they were able to define themselves as students. The research Claudia did with them was the catalyst for this change, demonstrating the power of teacher research to change both individual student behavior and school climate.[16]

ON TEACHING METAPHORS AND CARING

In *"I Won't Learn From You" and Other Thoughts on Creative Maladjustment*, Herb Kohl asks his readers to reflect on the images they have about teaching:

> Teachers in particular have an obligation to work to sustain hope and to resist giving up on young people. One way to do this is to remember why one decided to teach in the first place. What images and metaphors come to mind when teachers think about the original inspiration they felt and their desires to spend their lives working with young people?[17]

On the basis of this quote, I posed the following questions to the inquiry group at one of our meetings: How do you sustain hope and resist giving up on young people? Can you answer the question he asks with your own images and metaphors? It wasn't until almost the end of our year together, when I asked the group participants to write a piece called "A Letter to New Teachers," that this question was answered, by Junia Yearwood. Her metaphor for teaching was gardening, and this serves as a fitting analogy for the caring about which we have been reflecting in the preceding pages.

Teaching as Gardening

JUNIA YEARWOOD

Dear New Teacher,

I am a passionate gardener. In the spring and summer, I parade around my yard tending and enjoying my peonies, roses, and daffodils. From September to June, I roam around my classroom and the corridors of my school making sure that Tiffany, José, and Rasheed grow, mature, and bloom to their full potential as students and as citizens. *I am a year-round gardener.*

One important discovery I've made from many years of cultivating flowers and minds is that they all respond best to hands that tend them with faith, hope, and love. Without these three, my seedlings wilt; my flowers droop; my students languish; and I, the gardener, fail.

When I plant my seeds, I believe without a doubt that they will grow. I have no evidence that these particular seeds will grow, but I am firm in my belief that they will. Without that strong conviction, my efforts would be tenuous at best. I know that they will grow because they are seeds and under the right conditions—soil, water, and sun—seeds grow. My students grow also. I believe that all students have the ability to grow, to learn, under the right conditions. I know that they will rise to my expectations just as my clematis vine sprouts and climbs to whatever height I set my trellis; or as Mike Rose so succinctly affirms in his book *Lives on the Boundary*, "Students will float to whatever bar you set."[18]

My faith in my students is an extension of the confidence I have in myself as a person and educator. Maintaining my sense of self and the confidence I have in my skills is a continuous and never ending process. I work at it.

I garden because I love plants and flowers. I love to watch them grow and spread and fill in the brown patches of my yard with vibrant greens and rainbows of vivid colors. My love for plants is expressed in diverse and active ways:

- I love them enough to water and fertilize
- I love them enough to trim and prune
- I love them enough to divide, separate, and transplant
- I love them enough to leave alone and wait
- I love them enough not to overwater or overfeed

I garden in my classroom with the same love and care as I do in my yard. I say "I love you" to my students in many different ways:

- I love them enough to praise and encourage
- I love them enough to reprimand and discipline
- I love them enough to allow time to grow and develop
- I love them enough to keep myself intellectually alive
- I love them enough to give the same respect that I demand
- I love them enough to be unbiased and fair-minded
- I love them enough to expect the best
- I love them enough to demand the best

I am not a perfect gardener. In spite of all my faith, hope, and love, many of my plants do not thrive and flourish. My method of gardening, my lack of skills, and the environment that I create are a few of the possible reasons that some of my charges fail to respond. However, I keep cultivating. I am aware of my limitations, but my faith is unshaken. I hope that at some point another gardener will succeed in bringing Rasheed, Tiffany, or José to life just as I've been known to breathe the breath of life back into the near-to-death spider plants and Boston ferns that one of my colleagues keeps sending to my classroom.

I mourn when I lose a plant. I mourn because it was such a waste—a waste of potential, a waste of beauty, a waste of life. My grief, however, is tempered with a sense of reality. What's real is that some of my plants arrive broken, damaged beyond repair by some former gardener whose inflicted injury I could not mend and whose brand of gardening I try hard not to duplicate.

Dear New Teacher, welcome to my garden. Are you ready?

Junia Yearwood

"A FUNDAMENTAL BELIEF" IN STUDENTS

What does it mean to have what Steve Gordon once called a "fundamental belief in the lives and minds of students"? In his definition of a "passionate teacher," Robert Fried provides one answer to this question: "To be a passionate teacher," Fried writes, "is to be someone in love with the field of knowledge, deeply stirred by issues and ideas that challenge our world, drawn to the dilemmas and potentials of the young people who come into class each day—or captivated by all of these."[19]

As we have seen, teachers such as Junia Yearwood, Judith Baker, Claudia Bell, Ambrizeth Lima, and others who work in urban schools are passionate about teaching in just the ways that Fried articulates. Although they may work in difficult conditions and with young people who have

known little academic success, they—like many other excellent teachers—
have remained in teaching. At times disheartened because of scarce resources, overcrowded classrooms, lack of support, and other conditions
over which they have little power, these teachers nonetheless remain committed to their profession and especially to their students.

Talented teachers remain in teaching for many and varied reasons:
their own experiences in life, their profound belief in education, their political activism, and other motives that we will explore more fully in the
following chapters. But their "fundamental belief" in students is, for all,
the primary motivation. This means having faith in young people and in
their capacity and intelligence, in spite of conventional images and messages to the contrary. Affirming students' identities and lives and forming
caring relationships with them are some of the manifestations of this deep
faith. Every day, exceptional teachers in schools throughout the nation
tackle difficult circumstances in heroic but quiet ways. They do so by refusing to give in to the negative expectations that others may have of urban
schools or the children who study there.

Chapter 4

TEACHING AS HOPE AND POSSIBILITY

With contributions from Sonie Felix and Steve Gordon

Education happens when hope exceeds expectation. Teaching is what makes the difference.

Andy Hargreaves & Michael Fullan,
What's Worth Fighting for Out There?

In *The Dialectic of Freedom*, Maxine Greene writes, "My focal interest is in human freedom, in the capacity to surpass the given and look at things as if they could be otherwise."[1] The capacity, in fact, the *need* to look at things "as if they could be otherwise" is as good a definition of hope as I've seen. Hope explains why many teachers—in spite of the hardships and low status and working conditions—continue to teach.

Hope is at the very essence of teaching. In all my years of working with teachers, I have found that hope is perhaps the one quality that all good teachers share. Whether they teach in preschool or college, whether they teach math or art, good teachers have an abiding faith in the promise of education. This was also true of the teachers in the inquiry group. In spite of anger and impatience (we'll turn to these in the following chapter) or the level of frustration and exhaustion that they experienced, most remained in teaching, many for more than 20 years, because of hope.

In this chapter I explore the ways in which hope is manifested in teachers' work: optimism in the promise of public education and in their students; faith in their abilities as teachers; confidence in trusted colleagues and new teachers. In addition, I examine how hope is constantly tested. Most of the chapter is based on a conversation I had with a group of teachers at English High School, where both Junia Yearwood and Karen Gelzinis teach. It also includes the writing of two members of the inquiry group, Sonie Felix and Steve Gordon.

THE PROMISE OF PUBLIC EDUCATION

Most of us who've been educated in public schools in the United States, regardless of whether our experience was entirely positive or not, have an image of public schools as holding a noble purpose, a civic aim on behalf of the public good beyond individual advancement. This is our shared vision of what could be, and it explains the abiding faith and belief we have in the public schools.

That our public schools ever performed this admirable role for all citizens is questionable. In spite of John Dewey's idealistic assertion that "[i]t is the aim of progressive education to take part in correcting unfair privilege and unfair deprivation, not to perpetuate them," schools have regrettably too often served to uphold privilege.[2] In a provocative book on the history of public schools in the United States, Michael Katz demonstrated how from the very beginning they were "universal, tax-supported, free, compulsory, bureaucratically arranged, class-biased, and racist."[3] According to Katz, these seemingly contradictory features were interrelated and derived from the historic purpose of public schools: to train different segments of society for particular roles in life. Even if we do not accept the more deterministic aspect of Katz's thesis, there can be little argument that the outcome of public schooling has been unequal and unjust for certain segments of U.S. society.[4]

Teachers cannot ignore this disturbing history. Indeed, thoughtful, critical teachers have to reconcile values that at times seem irreconcilable: they have to combine an unshakeable belief that public education can lead to the opportunity for more choices and a better life with a healthy skepticism that challenges a simplistic correlation of education with progress. Those who tip the balance too much to one side can become indiscriminate defenders of the status quo; those who err too much on the other can turn into inflexible cynics unable to move forward. It takes some talent to find the right balance between hope and despair.

On a day when I visited Junia Yearwood's school, she gathered a small group of her most trusted colleagues and asked them to share their thoughts with me about my "burning question, *What keeps teachers going in spite of everything?* I spent a couple of hours talking with this diverse and inspiring group of teachers: Darryl Alladice, an African American literacy specialist who had taught in Boston for many years; Patrick Tutwiler, also African American, who was Junia's student teacher and a master's student at Harvard University; Juan Figueroa, a young Puerto Rican math teacher who had been teaching for a few years and who himself had been a student in the Boston public schools; Anita Preer, a White teacher who had taught for many years and was the faculty advisor for the school's news-paper; Mattie Shields, a veteran African American science teacher known for her calm and affectionate demeanor with students, and Karen Gelnizis, one of the teachers in the inquiry group.

It was obvious from this conversation that one of the great pillars of faith that kept some of these teachers in the profession was public educa-tion. Another related belief was that teachers could change lives. The deep sense of mission of these teachers was abstract (the very idea of public education) as well as concrete (the real lives of the young people they taught).[5] Early on in the conversation, Darryl explained,

> I go back to [my high school] where a high school teacher saved my life by giving me a book without having *any* requirement whatsoever. Just said, "Read the book" and it was called *The Promised Land*. And that's the book that started the road to reading. Once I started reading, I started seeing things differently. I started looking at maps, at street corners, and parks, and cities and states and the world. I just started reading and my horizons just became much more broad than they had been at the time. I was 17 years old. I was a pretty illiterate 17-year-old. I mean, I could spell, I could read math and stuff like that, but I wasn't reading. I wasn't understanding what I was reading.
>
> I was public schooled. I grew up in public schools. My aunts and uncles are all teachers and principals and professors at colleges. I come out of a family where we believe in public schooling, especially coming out of the 1960s. My family is from the South. We moved to the North, migrated to the North and public school is what we had. Public school can work. That's what got me started. That's what keeps me going, the belief that public schools can work. Cities can work. America can work.

Juan Figueroa echoed this statement, but with a slight difference. For him, it was seeing students graduate and succeed that was most motivat-ing. Although he had only been teaching for a few years, he had already had this experience:

> [What keeps me going is] seeing students that we've had here gradu-ate, go on to college, and know and stay in contact with them and you know what they're doing and where they're going. . . . I was lucky enough to teach, for a couple of years, a class of seniors. This is the first year where they'll be actually seniors, graduating from college. Knowing that they're going to be graduating this year, and that two of

them are going to be teachers—that is definitely, like, incredible! It's incredible that they will be coming back to a profession that I love and that they'll be doing the same thing.

At the end of the conversation, Junia Yearwood said, "I get so much energy from my kids, I really do. I think we all draw from our kids."

Some teachers have an enduring faith in public education because their schooling gave them the opportunity to escape from a life of poverty and desperation. Sonie Felix, a member of the inquiry group, came to the United States from Haiti as a young child of 6. At 26, she was the youngest teacher in the inquiry group. In response to my request for her teacher autobiography, she wrote not only her personal story, but also a moving declaration of her faith in the power of education. It is a good example of what Herb Kohl calls "hopemongering."[6]

Education Was My Way Out

SONIE FELIX

I was born on July 18, 1974, on the beautiful island of Haiti. I moved to Boston in the early 1980s and have lived here ever since. When I first arrived in the United States, I felt as if I had entered a different planet. Everything around me was strange and enormous. The people reminded me of animals, with their funny talk and robotlike walk, and the buildings stood like soldiers in the street.

It was my first time ever being away from my mother and my family. I felt alone and confused. I was much too young to understand why my parents had sent me away. I often wondered if I had done something wrong to deserve this, or maybe they just didn't love me anymore. All I knew is that I missed my family terribly and I didn't have any friends.

It wasn't until years later that I realized why my parents sent me away. They wanted a better life for me than the one they had to offer in Haiti. And the only way for me to obtain that lifestyle was through a good education. Although I did not agree with my parents' decision to send me away, as I reflect on my life today, I can truly say that they have given me a precious gift that I will always treasure. They provided me with the opportunity to get a good education. As years passed and I continued to work hard in school, it finally dawned on me how valuable an education really is.

It wasn't easy at first. There was the language issue. In order for me to do well in school, I had to learn how to speak English and communicate with my peers. Once I mastered that, there was the identity problem: Should I give up my culture and conform to the ways and the lifestyle of the United States? Or should I take pride in my heritage and alienate myself from my peers and become an outcast? I tried hard to camouflage my true feelings and disguise the war that was taking place inside of me by acting out in class and getting negative attention. But luckily for me, many of my teachers saw through the act and were able to guide me in the right direction. With my teachers' guidance, I was able to resolve many of the conflicts and at the same time excel in school. They taught me the valuable lessons that I hold dear to me to this day. They taught me that it was OK to be me and that education was my way out.

Education has been like a recurring theme in my life. The more I tried to escape it, the more it became a part of me. As I made my way through college, I began to fall in love with learning. The more I read, the freer I became. It was as if a sense of liberation swept over me and showed me the endless possibilities that were waiting for me. Through reading, I was able to free up my mind and my spirit. I read books by authors who, like myself, struggled to make it in America. They wrote about their hardships and how education helped them to overcome the obstacles that stood in their way. I read about the slaves who were denied an education and how they longed for a chance to be educated, some even risking their lives to attain it. Then I thought about my parents in my country and how they too saw the importance of learning and then it became clear to me what my purpose here on earth was. I knew right then and there what I wanted to do with my life: I wanted to teach.

Teaching to me involves more than just disseminating information to students and passing tests. It involves love, commitment, dedication, and patience. In order to teach, teachers must have faith in their students and believe in them. It cannot be just another job where you punch in at 7:00 and leave at 2:00. It is not easy being a teacher, but I believe that one has to be passionate about teaching and learning in order to teach our children.

In all of the chaos and confusion that has taken place in this system, I sometimes feel that my students and I are placed in a dark, dismal hole with a speck of light to guide us. As a teacher, it is my job to show the students that light, as dim as it may be, and let them know that bigger and better things are waiting for them on the other side. To give up now would be ludicrous. I know that my students need me now more than ever, and I need them too. All they need is a fair chance and someone to believe in them the same way my teachers believed in me. The best way that I can thank my teachers for the difference they have made in my life is by continuing the wonderful job they started. They instilled in me a love for learning and I, in turn, plan to share that with my students.

FAITH IN THEIR OWN ABILITIES AS TEACHERS

Excellent teachers have tremendous faith in their own abilities, but at the same time they lose sleep trying to find just the right approach or the lesson or book that will reach students who might seem at times "unreachable." In our interview, Darryl Alladice described how, as a teacher, he wanted to "fix things":

> I'm always looking for ways to fix it. I mean, I'll go home frustrated and I'll say, "OK, I need to try this; I need to try that. . . ." I need to keep trying ways to fix it, to fix it. I think good teachers are concerned with good teaching and fixing stuff and not just letting things happen, not letting it go. I think there's a conscious effort there. It's like playing ball. There's a conscious effort there to make the right pass, the no-look pass. . . . What novel will reach this kid? I'm always passing out novels in the hallways. I'll pass out the novel to this kid if I see him sitting in front of, let's say, the discipline office. I'll go in my office and I'll just say, "Here, read this.'" Because that's how it happened to me. I was that C-student. I was that jerk.

CONFIDENCE IN COLLEAGUES AND
THE NEXT GENERATION OF TEACHERS

Although most teachers don't have many school-sanctioned opportunities to meet with colleagues to prepare classes or talk about the latest research or just to try out ideas they've been playing with, some teachers nevertheless make the time to do these things in other ways. In spite of the limited time they have on their hands, some teachers join inquiry groups and professional organizations; they attend and participate actively in conferences; they present workshops together; and, in a myriad of other ways, they demonstrate that collegiality is essential for good teaching. For them, having colleagues in whom they can trust is one of the ingredients that keeps them in teaching.

In the work I've done with teachers, it has often been the case that their greatest inspiration comes from other teachers, not from outside "experts," certainly not from staff meetings, not even from books. These things may also inspire teachers, but it's puzzling out the day-to-day problems with colleagues that tends to be most helpful. I saw this clearly when I interviewed teachers at Karen Gelzinis's school. Karen, who admired several of her colleagues deeply, singled out Mattie Shields (Shields, a teacher of

22 years, said that she always returns to teaching because "this is where I should be"). Karen asserted, "My goal, when I grow up, I want to be like Mrs. Shields." This kind of respect for colleagues was clear throughout my time with the inquiry group. In fact, when I asked the small group of teachers I met with at Karen's school what their greatest satisfaction from teaching was, Mattie said,

> The greatest satisfaction I've gotten from teaching is really meeting wonderful colleagues like Mrs. Gelzinis, just being able to do it with really nice people. Really wonderful people, just gems in the field of education. People that when you speak, they hear you. It's not like they've never been in a classroom before or are from some planet or someplace and don't know what you're talking about.

For teachers who do not have this kind of support, the task may seem overwhelming. For those who do, teaching is made a little easier, a little more manageable. Most of the teachers in this particular group belonged to the same cluster, and just like an old married couple who had lived a good life together, they were comfortable with one another, even finishing one another's sentences, as we see in the following exchange. First Karen Gelzinis spoke:

> And that's one of the things that keeps us going. Like in this school, we'll often say that, if we weren't teaching together in the cluster, could we even have stayed sometimes in this school? But it's like we're in our own little world up here.

Junia Yearwood added,

> You really do need to find spaces to work. . . . As I say to people, I have found my space. And it's where I want to be.

Karen continued,

> And you know what people you need to be around to help you in your work. . . . So that's one of the things that helps you keep going too. It's just that support that you get from each other.

Junia concluded,

> Because if you had to come in every morning and all you heard was just negative, negative, negative . . . oh! I wouldn't even get out of bed.

Anita Preer, another of the teachers I interviewed that day, was an experienced and highly respected teacher who was the advisor for the school newspaper. Because of a number of difficult situations at school, it had been a very tough year emotionally. Anita said it was new teachers who gave her a thread of hope to cling to. She explained,

> What keeps me going is having a student teacher every year. That is what really keeps me going because I am able to recapture in this new person the idealism that I started with. You know, I have 28 years in the system and I'm very burned out, OK? This year has been particularly difficult because I lost a girl that I'd had since 10th grade that I loved like a daughter . . . that we lectured and, with all of the problems that inner-city kids have, she overcame it and went on to college and was motivated. It was a difficult year. It was a year when I was thinking that no matter what you do, no matter how hard you work, no matter how you pour yourself in, you can't change the inevitable. That's how I felt. I'm having a low year. I'm picking up, though. I'm picking up.
>
> Because it seems that so many of the social problems that we cannot control defeat our children, OK? So I thought about it, what you said about what keeps you going, and it is the thought that I have a student teacher every year who wants to teach in the inner-city schools; who comes to me with idealism and with hope and with intelligence and with ideas of how to fix it. Lots of ideas of how to fix it, and energy, and looking at my profession, looking at me as a model of my profession, of a profession that he wants to go into. And that's what keeps me going. Because, then, I always get recharged and regenerated and do the teaching.

Darryl echoed Anita's sentiments by comparing having a student teacher to having a partner in the classroom.

> For me, it's good to have a partner. I usually tell my student teacher, "It's going to be a ride—wonderful, questionable at times, but we're partners in this classroom." I tell my partner to wear sneakers—you'll be on your feet a lot!—and it's a profession where you are going to be asked to give and give and give. And just when you realize that you *are* giving, you're going to be asked to give some more. That's usually what I say the first day. And buy yourself some Pepperidge Farm lemon cookies and that's what gets you through once in a while. Do things for yourself, keep a little corner for yourself. Yeah, that's a start.

At the same time that they get "recharged" with the new teachers coming into the profession, some teachers worry about how new teachers are being recruited. Karen Gelzinis talked about an article she had seen in a Boston newspaper that reported on a teacher recruitment day:

> In the paper, the mayor and the superintendent said, "We're looking for people who want to work 12 hours a day," and blah, blah, blah. . . . And I said, if they just listen to what they're saying! Is that what they really want to do to people? And, yeah, *we've* done it, and sometimes, you say, but *how* have we done it? But I don't want to leave [the profession] thinking that I haven't tried to make a difference for the people that are coming after. Because I'm tired of seeing people, after 4 or 5 years, saying, "I love to teach, but I can't do this anymore."

"YOU HEAL, YOU HELP, YOU LOVE . . ."

In a letter addressed to teachers, Paulo Freire wrote, "It is impossible to teach without the courage to love, without the courage to try a thousand times before giving up."[7] Hope is the catalyst for courage, and in the preceding pages teachers shared examples of where their great reserves of hope originate—from their students and colleagues and future colleagues, from their obsession with improving their craft, and, most deeply, from the very idea of public education and the possibilities it holds out.

Hope can conquer many fears, and it can endure even when there is little cause for optimism. I end this chapter with the words of Anita Preer because they express this idea better than any I have seen. Although it was obvious that the year had been a trying one for her, and in spite of the fact that she described herself as "burned out," Anita continued to believe in the same high purpose of education that she always had. Teaching, she said, was "a life's work that is very, very dignified and very high level because you grow every day, you learn every day, and you change people's lives. And I don't know what else there is."

As we saw, having a student teacher was what energized Anita every year, so I asked her what advice she'd give to a new student teacher in her school. Her response was one of the most moving I've heard any teacher give:

> I think I'd say, "Thank you for coming in." Every day, "Thank you! Thank you! Thank you for coming into the Boston public schools!

You really could be doing other things and make so much more money and have much better [working] conditions." But one thing I said when Chris [her student teacher] was talking about how all the student teachers, once they come in here, they're like, "I don't have a life anymore! I don't have a life!" And I said, "You know something? This *is* a life!" You come in, you grow, you learn, it's never the same, it's always different. You heal, you help, you love. What's wrong with that? Is that a life or is that a life?

Chapter 5

TEACHING AS ANGER AND DESPERATION

With contributions from Karen Gelzinis and Sonie Felix

Anyone can become angry. That is easy. But to be angry with the right person, to the right degree, at the right time, for the right purpose and the right way—that is not easy.

Aristotle

It is easy to understand why hope is one of the qualities that most sustains teachers in their work. It is more difficult to understand how anger fits in. In fact, one can easily conclude that anger has no place in education and certainly not among committed and excellent teachers. But in working with the inquiry group, I came to understand that hope and anger are really two sides of the same coin. Hope is what invigorates teachers who face their students with courage and commitment every day; anger is the common response when the utopian vision of public education is betrayed. It can be the hedge against complacency.

Although anger can motivate, it can also lead to desperation, and desperation can nearly destroy a teacher's resolve. In this chapter, you will see examples of both.

WHEN TEACHERS ARE ANGRY

Teachers are angry about the injustices their students have to endure; impatient with the seeming arbitrariness of "the system"; baffled by school policies that are made by people far removed from the daily realities of classroom life; indignant at being treated as if they were children. I was surprised by the depth of anger of the teachers in the inquiry group. Certainly, they weren't *all* angry, and they weren't *always* angry, and they weren't *uniformly* angry, but there was some level of anger evident among most of them. At

one of our meetings, Junia Yearwood explained, "Anger is one of the motivating factors in keeping you going, keeping that passion alive. So, it may
be a negative emotion, but for most of us, it is anger at the injustice. . . . Anger is what fuels you." I suppose I was surprised because if these teachers—
who are all unquestionably outstanding, devoted, and skilled—are angry,
how do less effective and committed teachers feel?

Ambrizeth Lima, who had recently decided to return to graduate
school for a doctoral degree, clearly had mixed feelings about leaving.
While she was excited about her upcoming graduate studies, she also hated
leaving "my kids." But she was angry about what happens to teachers with
hope and dedication and passion. During a discussion about Herb Kohl's
book *"I Won't Learn from You" and Other Thoughts on Creative Maladjustment*,
Ambrizeth said that reading it had made her realize she had been "malad-
justed" the entire time she had been teaching! She went on to say that she
appreciated Kohl for finding an elegant way to describe what she had been
feeling. For her, she said, "it was crying, yelling at people, you know, just
gnashing my teeth. . . . And I'm still mad at people and I won't talk to
them."

I don't want readers to confuse anger with complaining, because it
wasn't complaining that I heard from these teachers. They weren't making excuses or looking for an easy out, as Karen Gelzinis explained:

> Whenever you say anything, it's always that you're looking for the easy
> way. . . . It's that distrust. . . . When you have a kid in your class that you
> know doesn't belong there—yes, the kid makes your life hard and it
> makes every other kid's in the class life hard, but that kid is having these
> tremendous problems and that kid shouldn't be there right now. And
> you say, "This kid is dying in front of me and I can't stand to watch him
> die anymore." You know, [they think] you're looking just to get rid of the
> kid and that's not it.

The inquiry group members did not want to be confused with teachers who complain but do not work, the kind of teachers described by one
of the members of the group as "those teachers who bring up all these issues all the time, but don't do anything in the classroom because they can't
focus on the teaching." They were speaking about teachers who hand out
nothing but ditto sheets as the extent of their daily lesson plan; who sit in
the faculty lounge and complain about their students' laziness and lack of
intelligence; who gripe about families that don't care; who romanticize
about how much better things were in some mythical "before." It should
come as no surprise that teachers such as these, that is, those who are least
successful, end up blaming students and parents for their failure.[1] But this

was clearly not the case with the inquiry group teachers. The teachers in the inquiry group knew their students as persons, in all their vulnerability, talent, and strength, not just in terms of the skills they lacked. They had faith in their students and believed they were intelligent and capable. They also believed in their own abilities as teachers. In all the time I spent with them, I never heard them speak a disparaging sentence about their students that began with the generalized *these kids*.

Other teachers with whom I have worked over the years were also angry, and it was my work with the inquiry group teachers that allowed me to see this. I learned that sheer anger and frustration can sometimes nurture teachers' determination. At one point, Ambrizeth Lima stated that she used to get angry with many of her colleagues, but that now "I'm learning that not everybody has to think the way I do. . . . It could be old age," she laughed (she was 36), "a sign of maturity. I have to accept that people feel as strongly as I do. . . . But I'm getting better at it; I'm learning to keep my mouth shut sometimes," she said. But Steve Gordon, another inquiry group participant, cautioned, "Don't get too good at it!" because, according to him, *it was important not to forget the anger*. Although they recognize the need to move beyond it, for some teachers anger serves to remind them why their role in society is so crucial. In spite of the constant restructuring, lack of respect, and indignities they suffer, issues we consider later, teaching remains a noble profession. It is righteous anger that sometimes helps remind teachers of this fact.

BUREAUCRATIC RESTRUCTURING

One reason for teachers' anger is the steady, perplexing changes they experience throughout their careers. Veteran teachers live through a constant barrage of "restructuring" and "reform" that arrives with each new wave of power, either in the central office of the school system or in the city or state in which they happen to teach. During the time when I met with the inquiry group, a hot topic of conversation was the latest version of change that had happened, the far-ranging Massachusetts Educational Reform.[2] The reform legislation had brought with it expectations about what "all students should know and be able to do"; new curriculum frameworks to help guide the effort; and a statewide assessment, the MCAS (Massachusetts Comprehensive Assessment Reform), to make sure it was succeeding.

Educational reform in Massachusetts had begun in the early 1990s as a progressive effort shared among many constituents: the Massachusetts legislature, the board and staff of the Massachusetts Department of Education, a progressive and highly collaborative state board of education, and hundreds of educators and citizens around the state. But after the 1992 elections, when the political winds had shifted sharply to the right, the new commissioner of education reconstituted the board, and decisions on policy, curriculum, and assessments became more ideologically driven and centralized. Thus, rather than being a comprehensive assessment, as had been promised, the MCAS became a high-stakes test and the major assessment of progress for all 4th- 8th- and 10th-grade public school students. The 10th-grade MCAS was to be used within a few years as a graduation requirement. High school teachers, particularly those who taught 10th grade, would be the teachers most affected by this change. All the teachers in the inquiry group would feel the impact one way or another.

It was hard to find a teacher among those in the inquiry group who did not support rigorous, demanding standards for their students. More than anyone else, these teachers knew firsthand that there had been few demands placed on urban students in the past. Because of this, some of them had placed enormous faith in the new reform effort. But as time went on, their support waned. They envisioned disastrous results (wholesale failure among their students and even higher drop-out rates than before) if the sole criterion for progress was to be the MCAS. The focus of the reform effort had shifted. Whereas previously the emphasis had been on high standards for all students, with appropriate resources to help them achieve those high standards, now standardization through high-stakes testing was stressed. Further, teachers in the inquiry group often found the curriculum content of the standards limiting, narrowing the kind of in-depth work they wanted to do with their students. Because it was frequently based on little more than rhetoric, this kind of standardization angered the teachers. Steve referred to it one day when he wrote about the hopes and fears his students' parents might express: "'Will my child achieve and find dignity in a world which has denied learning?'" The school system, he maintained, offered the parents and their children only what he called "the secular frauds: the Stanford [test]; MCAS; rubrics; 'best practices.'"

Constant restructuring can lead to bureaucratic changes, but sometimes little else. Resentment at this kind of change is a major reason for the anger that some teachers feel. The teacher autobiography that Karen Gelzinis shared at a meeting of the inquiry group vividly illustrates this:

The More Things Change . . .

KAREN GELZINIS

Somehow, I always felt that I was a teacher, not just because I was the oldest of eight, but even before that. When we played on our street, it was often school. We had three porches attached to my grandmother's triple-decker [house]. As I think of it, we had more space then than some of the teachers in my school do now—and we had supplies. . . . And on those porches, I taught.

I loved real school when I finally got there. There was magic. Our classes had 48 kids but I always felt special there. . . . I always loved it. I went to parochial school, and I would just watch everything that my teachers did, every move that they made, and I just wanted to do what they did because I felt that they made magic.

In school, I got chances to teach other kids. When I was in the sixth grade, we had a girl come to our school from China who spoke little English and because I knew what I was supposed to know, I got to tutor her in English. . . . Then when we were in high school (this was in the late '60s) another nun came to live at our convent. She was doing a survey of the Puerto Rican kids in Boston who were out of school [; her name was] Sister Frances Georgia.[3] She talked our nuns into letting us out of class [for] a period near the end of the day to go down to the middle of the D Street Projects to tutor. . . . So they let us teach. We taught the Puerto Rican kids English.

Then, after a while, on Sundays instead of going to a regular mass, we would go to Spanish mass held in South Boston. It was just wonderful because I went from these masses, where the priest was there [in front] and all the people were [just listening], to these [Spanish] masses where there was just so much hugging and singing and we just fell in love with it. That's when I also found out how racist we were because the reason why mass was being held there was because they—whoever "they" was—didn't want to have Spanish mass in the "regular" church. Some people said it was because [Puerto Rican] people would feel more comfortable there, but as time went on, you learned that that wasn't really the reason.

I got to know a lot of the kids, I got to know a lot of the families. I lost a boyfriend because I was hanging around with all these Puerto Rican kids. . . . My father was afraid that something terrible was going to happen [to me], but we just didn't listen to him and so it was just a wonderful experience.

I was going to be a math major. I had been accepted for early admission at Emmanuel [College] and after doing this tutoring, I decided in June of my senior year that I was going to be an elementary [school] teacher, and all my teachers flipped out: "You don't know what you're doing!" [they said]. But I knew what I was doing.

I started teaching elementary school in the Boston public schools. The first day of school, I was called to the Christopher Gibson School, which is [in] *Death at an Early Age* in Kozol's book. . . .[4] It was 5 years after Kozol had been there. I was called the first day of school, like they used to do in Boston, wait until the last minute to call people. . . . It was a fifth-grade class. Actually, I was "subbing" for the assistant principal who was pulled out because, just like in Kozol's book, a school had burned in the summer so there were two schools in the [building] again. So he was trying to manage two schools in this one elementary school. [When] I got there, he said, "Your room is down there in the corner." I went down there, the kids were already there, and with *nothing*. It was just like being on the porches again: You just taught.

Then the next year, it was the start of desegregation and the day before school opened (after I decorated the room and everything!) I got a call saying, "We want you to go to a fifth grade in West Roxbury." That was like foreign to me, even though I had grown up in an all-White neighborhood. I went out to West Roxbury, but this wasn't the same kind of White that I had grown up with: Nobody on the street, kids even didn't know who lived next to them and all. It was the first year of busing so I had kids from Dorchester, mostly Black kids, a lot of kids from Montserrat. . . .

Then the next year, I taught at St. Joseph's Community School in Roxbury [a Black community]. I was a Chapter 1 teacher. It was a community-controlled school; I think it still is.[5] There were two nuns who were White, and two Chapter 1 teachers who had arrived from Boston public schools and we were White, and the whole rest of the other teachers were Black. That was really a great experience because I felt what it was like to be the only one. . . . But it was also a kind of psycho period because I was leaving South Boston every day. . . . and the mounted police would be rushing up and crazy people would be coming up to the school to yell at the buses.[6] And I would be going to St. Joseph's, where we would start school by singing the Black National Anthem, and it was all Black identity. . . .

My whole 27 years [in the Boston public schools] have been about change. You know, the Gibson School 5 years before [I got there] was turned upside down when Kozol wrote his book, but when I got there, everything was just the way it had been before the book. Then there was desegregation and everything was turned upside down. We had magnet schools. Where are they now? . . . Now that's all gone and then here comes the whole assignment of students. It just disappears like a "poof." And it's like, wait a minute, people *cared* about what was going on in the classroom, we did all that stuff.

Karen Gelzinis's story was not only compelling, it also provided a living history of changes in the Boston public schools over the past 30 years. The deeper she got into the story, the angrier she became. Karen is a caring, devoted teacher, but at times she wondered if there was any rhyme or reason to what goes on in urban schools with poor children.

THE NATURE OF "THE SYSTEM"

The very nature of the school system is sometimes baffling, leaving teachers bewildered and at a loss as to how to fight. Sometimes they feel as if they might suffocate under the weight of all the rules and regulations. Sonie Felix once said, "School is like a jail. I feel like breaking out."

Anger at the arbitrary nature of "the system" is evident as we continue with Karen's story. For an early meeting of the inquiry group, I had asked teachers to write down their "burning question," that is, the issue they wanted to focus on for the duration of our inquiry group so that these questions could become part of our agenda. Karen, however, was concerned that we might lose sight of the original question that had brought us together in the first place, the *What keeps teachers going?* question. The response she sent to my request is one of the angriest and most heartbreaking pieces of writing I've read from a teacher.

On Homemade Protractors and the Will to Fight

KAREN GELZINIS

The initial question raised by Sonia, "What keeps teachers going in spite of everything?" is the question that drew me to the group and keeps gnawing at my soul.

At our first meeting in June, I saw all these faces around the table, people with whom I had shared chunks of time in my life: a new teacher who taught across the hall from me; a teacher who was in a master's degree program with me (we were trained to be generic specialists—the BPS [Boston public schools] /federal government even picked up the major cost of the courses we attended during summers and several school years. This was no "put-in-your-time, pick-up-your-degree" program; we had to produce/defend a master's thesis. I have the bound copy to show for this time, as well as the increased pay. But the system never used us as generic specialists. What keeps us believing, putting in the time?); the aunt of a former student; my student/now teacher with whom I spent her first year in high school, as well as her first year as a teacher [Sonie Felix]; colleagues with whom (for the first time since 1973), I've had ongoing conversations about this process called learning/teaching, whom I credit/blame for arousing within me the questions. What am I doing here? Are we so dedicated, or are we so sick, to keep at it in a system that says one thing, but almost never backs it, the kids, or us up?

Before Christmas, I picked up the Sizers' book, *The Students Are Watching*.[7] I have not opened it. I can't get beyond the title; it stays in my mind. I know they are watching. They are watching and seeing . . . everything—they see the computer strips and no computers, and now each morning, the kids who come in early see us cleaning off the desks, cleaning off the broken pieces of ceiling tiles, the mouse droppings which fell the night before as the electricians install the new wiring for the new Internet hookups for the new computers which we don't have. They see these electricians coming in as they are working after school with the protractors and centimeter rulers I've xeroxed on transparency film, along with the xeroxed graph paper. They laugh when I give out the protractors and rulers, and they tell me that I'm a trip. When I check their binders at the end of each term, I see those cheap, "homemade" protractors and rulers with holes punched in them, right in the front of the binders, and I want to cry. And each year, sophomores, juniors, and seniors will come back and tell me that they still use their protractor, or they ask if I have another one.

In a writing group, the question was posed, What do we do for us, to keep our batteries charged, so that we can do our best for our students? A teacher wrote that this is a major problem and that she'll often take a shower when what she really needs is a nice, long bubble bath, because she doesn't have time. Everyone in the group knew exactly what she was talking about. So what (or who) keeps us on this crazy treadmill? The kids who are watching . . .

Last week, in an article on restructuring, another book was mentioned and now that title, too, keeps going through my head: *What's Worth Fighting for Out There?*[8] All discussions about restructuring should start with this question. I don't fight; I'm too busy making protractors. I don't fight; I don't want to have to leave my kids, my school. I don't fight . . . and I'm getting angrier at those who don't see that schedules and other superficial changes don't restructure schools (really); it's the relationships that transform. I don't fight . . . and the students are watching.

What is so reinforcing that it keeps this seemingly irrational behavior going? I can teach something with a pencil and a piece of paper (and sometimes a plastic ruler or sometimes with just a good example) and a kid will get it, and they tell me that they understood something that they never understood before. And I don't fight, because *this* is what it's all about. But the system doesn't change, while it is ever changing, "ever restructuring," ever ignoring the relationships. What's worth fighting for in my school? The students are watching.

INDIGNITY AT THE LACK OF RESPECT

Teachers resent being treated like children, and they become incensed at the lack of respect they are shown by administrators. The reluctance of administrators to involve teachers more substantively in school reform efforts is certainly not a new problem.[9] In the case of the teachers in the inquiry group, several mentioned being consulted about schedule and other changes in the school only to have their suggestions completely ignored when the changes were made. If teachers protested, according to Karen Gelzinis, they were told, "Stop complaining and get on with your lives." She responded, "But, you know, teaching *is* our lives, and so we *can't* stop!"

The general public's disregard for the professional and intellectual abilities of teachers is another sore point. There is a widespread belief, for example, that teacher education students, and teachers in general, are simply not as smart as other professionals. Yet the data do not confirm this belief.[10] Related to this, the idea that teaching takes skill and intelligence is not broadly shared. One reason is that, at the beginning of the 20th century, when primary schooling became widely available to children in the United States, most teachers were recruited from among the ranks of young unmarried women.[11] Teaching thus became linked in the popular imagination with "women's work," and the idea that it takes little more than common sense and good instincts is difficult to dispel.

The lack of respect for teachers' work, and for their judgment, was never more evident to me than in a conversation I had with a group of teachers one day. Anita Preer, one of those teachers, addressed the difference between appreciation and respect and what it would mean if administrators were to have real respect for teachers. She was particularly incensed one day that "outside experts" were brought in to help redesign the school, while teachers had not been asked for their suggestions:

> Because they'll say, "Oh, Anita, I appreciate all that extra work you do. Don't you know that? Do you think I don't appreciate your work?" [But] it's not appreciation [I want], it's having *respect* for your work, the quality of your work, for the standard of your work, for the contributions that you make. . . . You think some 26-year-old twerp who doesn't know anything should be redesigning the school and telling me what I'm going to teach and what Karen is going to teach, not respecting our expertise?

Teachers' anger and frustration in such situations is palpable. Talking and laughing about it, as those teachers did that day during our conversation, can provide some relief. But when anger crosses over to desperation, it is not easy to move forward.

DESPERATION

The question that Karen Gelzinis addressed in the previous section, What's worth fighting for? comes up often in teachers' conversations. Their first answer is invariably the same: students, especially those who have been deserted by other teachers, by the schools they attend, or by society. These are the students who have least benefited from education. For some teachers, such as Karen Gelzinis, the most difficult and rebellious of the students are especially worth fighting for. Karen appreciated what she called the "insurrectionists" among her students because, although she herself had never been rebellious as a child, she relished the rebel spirit in her students: "I don't know about anybody else, but I was always quiet [in school], like 'Yes, Sister,' 'No, Sister.' And so when I started teaching, I loved those kids who said, 'No, I'm not going to do this,' because I was never brave enough to say it. So I always love those kids."

One of those kids was Sonie Felix. Sonie had been a student of Karen's in high school, about 13 years earlier. She was a rebellious student and a source of both exasperation and joy for Karen. During her years in high school, Sonie was just as likely to excel in school as to end up in detention for some infraction or other. But in spite of all her visits to detention, and to Karen's great delight and excitement, Sonie became a teacher. As we saw in the previous chapter, Sonie wrote eloquently about the promise of public education. In September when she had written that "education was my way out," she had seemed unstoppable, a young teacher blazing with energy and hope. That day, she had said, "To give up now would be ludicrous." But by April, she was thinking of quitting.

The initial question Sonie had said she wanted to explore as her burning question had to do with her students' lives outside school. She had thought about interviewing them to find out how school could connect more effectively with their home and community lives. But she came into our April meeting with something else on her mind. She said, "Now I'm at a point where it's not about *them* anymore but about *teaching*, period." She then read something she had written the night before that obviously had been on her mind for some time. There was scattered initial nervous laughter when she read the title of her piece, but the room soon became still when everyone realized that Sonie was very serious. As she read her essay, she sobbed quietly and had to stop from time to time.

Considering Retirement at 26

SONIE FELIX

Having taught in the Boston public school system for 5 years now, I am debating over whether or not I want to continue this line of work. I have been pondering over this question for years and it seems as though the deeper I get into the field of education, the more I learn about the injustices that teachers are put through. It's as if the system is sucking the life out of you and then asking you to focus on children and teach them. It's almost as if the system is forcing you to quit.

Let me first start off by saying that I enjoy teaching and I believe it is my calling. I also love my students. But the system does not provide me with the support or the opportunity to grow as an individual. Everything is always rushed. This didn't happen overnight, just up in my head. It was a slow agonizing process. It's like an infected sore that spreads through the body and eventually reaches the brain and forces you to become sick of everything. It's easy to say that if you reach that point in any job, then just quit. But what happens when that job is your life and calling? What do you do then? In the book *"I Won't Learn From You" and Other Thoughts on Creative Maladjustment,* Kohl states that "[t]eachers in particular have an obligation to work to sustain hope and resist giving up on young people." I believe that the obligation does not rest in the hands of teachers solely, but there are numerous people who play a role in shaping students' learning.

Does quitting mean that you have to give up on young people? Is there a way to build communities and climates within a corrupt system that supports and encourages teachers to continue their important work? Is it possible to create other options besides quitting?

MOVING BEYOND THE ANGER

Reading this chapter, you might think that being a caring, competent teacher means you need to be perpetually angry. Is this the case? I do not believe it is. After all, the motivations that brought this group of teachers into teaching in the first place were based on hope, care, generosity, and a sense of purpose—a belief in the promise of public education, a faith in the capability and intelligence of young people, enthusiasm for teaching and learning, and a passion for social justice. These are all positive forces. Yet anger seems so negative and self-defeating, especially when it becomes the kind of anguish that Sonie described.

Rather than become complacent with the situation, most of the inquiry group teachers were able to *move beyond the anger*. Concerned that we were spending too much time complaining, Judith Baker said, "Bitching and moaning is not going to change my practice and bitching and moaning is not going to help the kids." Moreover, inquiry group teachers didn't use the poverty or other problems the students faced as a reason to expect any less of them. In spite of the conditions in which the students lived, the teachers had faith in their abilities. Judith explained that she wanted us to focus on academic issues, adding, "I would exclude all 'social work' remedies. This is typical talk that teachers always do that leads nowhere." Junia noted, "What I try to keep focused on is my kids, the students. They keep me going." She added:

> I am very much aware of all the other problems and I deal with them every day. Problems with administrators: I have my problems and I share all of those problems. But *I cannot be effective in a classroom if I take them in with me.* And I choose not to, OK? So, I'll come to meetings like this and I'll talk about it, but I don't go to school and talk politics and get all riled up about that because [then] I'll never get anything done in the classroom. . . . If I have to say something, I'll say it. And if I have to fight for my kids for anything, I do that valiantly. But I'm talking about getting caught up in [the politics] at the expense of [the kids]. I see a lot of people do that. They get caught up.

Anger, then, is not always a negative emotion, especially if it is motivated by a deep caring for students, a hope for the future, and a vision of how it could be otherwise.

POSTSCRIPT

Sonie Felix is still teaching.

Shortly after the meeting in April when she announced she was thinking of leaving teaching, Karen Gelzinis, Sonie's former teacher, called her, and they spoke at length. Karen gave Sonie the kind of advice and support that only another teacher who understands what it means to abandon one's "calling," as Sonie described it, can give.

When we first started meeting as an inquiry group, I could see the impatience in Sonie's eyes. She wasn't shy about expressing her frustration, either. She would ask, What are we going to *do*, and what would be our *product*? Were we just going to *talk*? Wasn't this a waste of time? By our last meeting, during the retreat we held in May, her words had changed considerably. Sonie had developed not only a desire, but indeed a *need*, to talk. At the end of the meeting, she thanked all her colleagues for their help and for participating in the inquiry group. She said,

> I think that these conversations are important in terms of continuing with teaching. I think if we omit these conversations, that *that's* how and why people tend to leave, because these conversations don't happen. They're not common. So, it was really insightful and it gave me strength to look at what I was doing and to want to continue.

There was a brief silence and then I asked, "So, are you staying?" She immediately answered, to the applause and laughter of her colleagues, "Of course," adding, "I don't have a choice." Sonie decided to return the following year in spite of the problems she had so painfully articulated. She has been teaching for over 2 years since that time, and she has begun to work with another inquiry group.

Chapter 6

TEACHING AS INTELLECTUAL WORK

With contributions by Patricia Bode and Stephen Gordon

If schools are to be places that encourage new teachers, causing them to see teaching as an interesting and unique career, they have to be intellectually and socially challenging environments in which teachers read together, reflect on practice, develop curriculum with a local, situated quality, and become conscious about the development of a learning community.
Vito Perrone, *A Letter to Teachers: Reflections on Schooling and the Art of Teaching*

Good teachers think deeply and often about the craft of teaching and the process of learning. They are not simply technicians who know how to write good lesson plans and use collaborative groups effectively, although this too is part of what they do. Above all, excellent teachers are engaged every day in *intellectual* work, the kind of serious undertaking that demands considerable attention and thought. They devote substantial time and energy to their teaching and, over time, they develop extensive expertise and confidence in the work they do. Henry Giroux has defined teachers as intellectuals in this way: "[I]n order to function as intellectuals, teachers must create the ideology and structural conditions necessary for them to write, research, and work with each other in producing curricula and sharing power. . . . As intellectuals, they will combine reflection and action in the interest of empowering students with the skills and knowledge needed to address injustices and to be critical actors committed to developing a world free of oppression and exploitation."[1]

All good teachers, whether they consciously carry out research or not, are researchers in the broadest sense of the word. This is because good teachers are also learners, and they recognize that they need to keep learning throughout their careers if they are to improve. They probe their subject matter, constantly searching for material that will excite and motivate their students; they explore pedagogy to create a learning environment that is both rigorous and supportive; they talk with their colleagues about difficult situations. Above all, they value the intellectual work that is at the core of teaching.

But teacher-intellectuals do not have all the answers, and they are rarely cocky about what they know. At times troubled about particular dilemmas in their classrooms or filled with doubt about what might be the best approach to use with their students, they are not shy about exploring these issues more deeply. The big and small dilemmas they encounter in their teaching become grist for the mill of their learning. This is the kind of teacher-researchers described by Marilyn Cochran-Smith and Susan Lytle as "architects of study and generators of knowledge."[2]

The intellectual work of teachers is apparent in many ways: through curriculum development, both individual and collaborative; through journal and other kinds of writing in which they engage, individually or collectively; through actual research projects they carry out in their classrooms; through attendance at conferences and active membership in professional organizations; and through workshops and other presentations that teachers themselves give. In this chapter, we focus on just two of these ways. First, we explore what Steve Gordon called "the need for adult conversations" by looking at examples of how teachers "do" intellectual work through dialogue. Second, we examine how Patty Bode, an art teacher in a middle school, and Steve, an English high school teacher, ponder what it means to develop curriculum that is both vital and scholarly.

THE NEED FOR ADULT CONVERSATIONS

Teaching can be the loneliest of professions. The job of teaching consists mainly of working with students for most of the day, and teachers are unable to connect with colleagues during the workday in any but the most superficial of encounters. As they run from one task to another, from office to classroom to hall duty to staff room, teachers barely have time to think. It is only when they return home, worn out after a full day, that they may be able to reflect on what happened. In these moments, sitting quietly or planning their work for the next day, they may ponder what took place during the day. Was the approach they used an effective way to teach the concept they wanted to get across? Did a particular reading they used that day have an impact on their students? What might have made a certain lesson more inviting? More specifically, they may wonder, Why didn't Margarita participate in class more fully? Or, Why does Terrance speak so eloquently but refuse to do homework? These are the kinds of questions that call for the longed-for but infrequent "adult conversations" Steve Gordon mentioned in one of our meetings—conversations about teaching, about the problems teachers face when they enter their classrooms, about their dilemmas and the resolutions to them. These kinds of conversations are, in the long run, what creates community among teachers.

My work with teachers over many years has convinced me that it is time to challenge the perception of teaching as a private effort. If teachers are to improve what they do and gain more satisfaction from their work, building critical and long-standing relationships with their colleagues is essential. In many schools where teaching is still considered a solitary craft with room for only idiosyncratic responses, a sense of community is missing. Benjamin Barber might have been pondering just such a problem when he wrote: "Perhaps it is time to start thinking about what it means to say that community is the beginning and the end of education—its indispensable condition, its ultimate object—and time, then, to do something about it in words and in deeds."[3]

During the meetings of the inquiry group and in spite of their weariness at the end of a full day of teaching, most of the teachers, after an initial winding down, participated spiritedly in our conversations. For most inquiry group members, talking about questions in teaching that mattered was a powerful validation of the importance of their work. These conversations are sadly missing in many schools, where meetings are devoted to the minutiae of running a school or the latest mandate from "downtown" or the state, rather than to big questions about curriculum, pedagogy, and the purposes of education.

But adult conversations, while necessary, can also be troubling. Dialogue alone does not solve problems, and it can in fact bring up more questions than solutions. One obstacle to true dialogue is that many teachers are reluctant to expose to others what they perceive to be their shortcomings. In this they are simply human; most of us need to establish a deep trust with colleagues before we are ready to expose our weaknesses. Yet many teachers do not have the opportunity to establish these trusting relationships with colleagues. In a comprehensive review of research on teacher learning, Suzanne Wilson and Jennifer Berne found a number of recurring patterns in even the most successful examples of professional development; these patterns reveal that "teachers enjoy the chance to talk about their work, that it takes time to develop a community, that teachers have very little experience engaging in a professional discourse that is public and critical of their work and the work of their colleagues."[4]

Another difficulty with engaging in dialogue, especially in urban schools, is that differences between students (primarily of "minority" backgrounds) and teachers (mostly of "majority" backgrounds) are often hidden but hard to ignore. Questions of race and social class are tough for many teachers to face, and if they come up in teachers' meetings, they tend to be ignored. This difficulty is being addressed more frankly than before in the literature on teacher learning.[5] But as a profession, and, even more important, as a nation, we have yet to become comfortable discussing race and other differences. Little wonder, then, that these remain disturbing topics of conversation for many teachers.

In spite of the complications involved in talking about, writing on, and puzzling over persistent dilemmas, however, the process can be uplifting and transformative. On the basis of their years of work with teacher-researchers, Marilyn Cochran-Smith and Susan Lytle came to the conclusion that "[w]hen groups of teachers have the opportunity to work together as highly professional teacher researchers, they become increasingly articulate about issues of equity, hierarchy, and autonomy and increasingly critical of the technocratic model that dominates much of school practice."[6] If teachers are to develop as intellectuals, having to engage in what may be disquieting dialogue is part of the price to be paid. In the end, this kind of dialogue (what Cochran-Smith describes as "hard talk") is a prerequisite both for developing the intellectual community that is desperately needed in schools and for imagining different possibilities for teachers and their students.[7]

THE CALL TO WRITE

It is no accident that many teachers use writing as a way to do their most important thinking about their craft.[8] For them, writing is not too different from thinking about their work in classrooms. This was certainly the case with some of the members in the inquiry group, who felt the need not simply to *talk* about what they were thinking and doing, but also to *write* about it. At one meeting, Steve Gordon described how writing about perplexing problems helped him figure them out. In response to a request that each of the teachers write to me about the problem they wanted to explore, he sent me an E-mail message using the example of a reading assessment to illustrate "the call to write."

Understanding Through Writing

STEPHEN GORDON

Dear Sonia,

Thank you for your encouragement about my writing. I want to try to understand what I have been doing for 30 plus years and what I do every day so that my work may be explicable to me and to others. Just last week, for example, I had to give a midyear reading assessment, the Scholastic Reading Inventory (SRI), to my students who had been designated in September "transition" students [indicating that they needed remedial work], based on their Stanford reading and math scores. I taught them in 2-week cycles since September. In October the city mandated that we give these students this SRI, giving it again midyear, and then a final time at the end of the year.

The first week of February I gave the test after "teaching" these students for about 10–12 weeks total, consisting of 2-week cycles. For one week I would not grade these tests. I just feared the results. What would students' [score] going up mean about my pedagogy? What would their [score] going down mean about my pedagogy? Was anyone equally interested in what I was doing in my classes with these students? Was anyone assessing whether my teaching decisions, my assignments and activities, my beliefs and instruction, arose from sound, principled commitment to these particular students? Was anyone interested as much in who these students were, namely, was there comparable discussion about my students' language, experience, beliefs about literacy, reading tests, school, teaching, as there was about the necessity of assessment? Reasoning by analogy, perhaps erroneously, would a doctor give follow-up tests if he did not believe that the treatment was likely to produce results?

My experience with teaching reveals that teaching does not rely on a cookbook from which one chooses recipes that "work." The incessant subtext of this is always that the teacher is responsible for succeeding alone, as if the recipes were enough, as if children were vegetables or meat having no individuality and history, unable to participate in their own "cooking."

I have marked the SRI test this weekend, and the scores of many students improved. A few did not; a few went down. And what am I to make of this? This is the poison. Either what I am doing is pedagogically sound, honoring the literacy lives and development of my students, or it is not. Who are we trying to impress by using this assessment? Where has this come from? Is it an inevitable result of a free enterprise society that is driven by the price of everything, having to compare products and people to ensure that someone is deficient?

The above does not really bring me to the reason for writing. I was supposed to write about "what I plan to work on." Maybe I want to document my struggle of how one teacher of a certain background, education and persuasion—and experience teaching urban students—tries to have his work, his teaching decisions, reflect, instantiate, embody, "represent" beliefs and "knowledge" about cognition, learning, literacy, psycholinguistics, sociolinguistics, pedagogy, politics.

Ideally, I should write every day around these issues: What did I do today, why and how was it principled, rational, reflective of some knowledge and belief? And what happened when I did it in my classroom? Upon rereading [this], it sounds too hard.

Looking forward to seeing you Thursday.

Steve Gordon

There is so little time for teachers to write; too many other demands on their time make writing a luxury that they think they can ill afford. But the call to write needs to be cherished because writing is one of the few ways in which teachers can use the space and time needed to think seriously about their craft. Writing about their teaching, especially if they share their writing with colleagues, is a public way of understanding and improving their work. Exploring questions through writing, therefore, also fulfills the passionate need that many teachers have for communion with others.

WRITING TO IMPROVE CURRICULUM

For teachers, writing serves many purposes. It is a place to rethink practice, consider alternatives to particular goals, or improve curriculum. All these purposes are served in the segment by Patty Bode that you are about to read.

Patty Bode has taught at all grade levels from preschool through eighth grade. Currently a teacher at a middle school, Patty has been a researcher since the first day she entered the classroom. For her, curriculum development itself is an art; it is not simply following someone else's lesson plan or relying on the research of others. Art classes, according to Patty, shouldn't be merely pleasant lessons where students make beautiful objects. Instead, art—like any other subject of study—needs to be viewed within a larger context. It is the only way children can learn about art in a way that will be both more meaningful and more critical. This explains why doing research before each lesson is so much a part of teaching for Patty. She can frequently be found on the Internet checking on a particular source, or developing a PowerPoint presentation for her lesson, or cutting up old art magazines in order to mount and frame photographs of artworks and craft objects from all over the world. She also connects these lessons to the other subjects her students are learning. Being fortunate to be part of a middle-school "team" that connects art with language arts, mathematics, social studies, and science, she is able to develop art lessons that are consequential to her students' learning.

Patty takes very seriously the responsibility to develop curriculum that educates and engages at the same time, opening students' eyes to new worlds that lie outside their own particular experiences. For Patty art is of necessity multicultural. In her room, we find examples of art from every continent and from scores of countries and cultures. Her students learn to question the supremacy of European art at the expense of others, and they learn to admire and respect both the art and the crafts of many different societies.

The following segment is a good example of teaching as intellectual work. In it, we catch of glimpse of the careful curriculum theorizing and planning that goes on before Patty actually teaches a lesson.

Puerto Rican Arts in a Social Context

PATTY BODE

"Can we make those?" my students call out, as we study the colorful *vejigante* masks of Puerto Rico in a video.

"Yes we can make these masks," I assure them. "Let's figure out what the vejigante mask is all about. That will help us build our own mask interpretations."

For each slide that flashes on the screen, I ask my students, "What do you notice? What do you wonder?"

Jasmina jumps in. "I notice lots of spots. They painted them with spots, on every mask. I wonder why?"

"I see lots of horns; I notice they are scary," Orlando calls out.

"I notice that each mask is different; some look kinda the same, but they are all different," Richie adds.

"I see fangs, teeth, horns, big mouths, and flared nostrils," Sarah adds. "I wonder how they made so many teeth on that one?"

The vejigante character from Puerto Rico is a crowd pleaser, both on the island during carnival, and here in Amherst, Massachusetts, in my middle school art room. But most of my students have limited knowledge of the arts of Puerto Rico or of the sociopolitical context of the history of Puerto Rico that is expressed through many of the arts. Exploring the history, traditions, and cross-cultural influences of the vejigante mask provides a context for understanding the intersection of Taino, European, and African cultures in the Caribbean. Art making in this context enhances a more comprehensive understanding of Puerto Rican arts, culture, and history. The following is a glimpse into the organic evolution of my art curriculum that started years ago with a well-intentioned—yet superficial—multicultural focus, and which continues to evolve and develop into a deliberate intent to teach about the Puerto Rican experience in a broader context.

I began to develop a curriculum about the vejigante years ago, but the more I worked on it, the more I began to question the image of Puerto Rico that my students were internalizing. Whether I asked students in first grade or seventh grade, in a follow-up lesson, what they could tell me about Puerto Rico, many students would say, "It's the island where they make vejigante masks!" Yes, that is true, but did they think that everyone on the island spent their time designing and wearing vejigante masks? Did they understand the specificity of this folk character to certain traditions, regions, and events? Would my students assume that "folk art" existed on the island in a void without any previous historical context? Was I denigrating this beautiful tradition to the status of a mere "tourist curriculum" by exploiting the attractive color and character of the custom? Did the students understand the significance of the intersection of Spanish and African cultures in the endearing character of the vejigante?

I firmly believe that folk arts need to be taught in the context of contemporary arts and fine arts: Did my students have a grasp on the contemporary art of Puerto Rico represented by scholars of the arts at the universities and art centers and by active artists in the museums and galleries of Puerto Rico? Did they see the connection between Puerto Rican artists in New York and throughout the United States to artists on the island? Did I give students the opportunity to step into the artists' work to see the thriving community and culture of Puerto Rico?

I heard many non–Puerto Rican students say things such as "Puerto Rico is a nice place to take a vacation." While this may be true, if that is all they know about Puerto Rico, they're missing a lot. Did students understand the relationship of the ecology of the island and its landscape to the political status? Do they understand the significance of programs such as the industrialization project called Operation Bootstrap in the 1950s, or of the U.S. military presence on Vieques today? Did my students gain any knowledge about the U.S. relationship with Puerto Rico and the island's long struggle against colonization? I hoped all my students were learning positive images of Puerto Rican culture and that my Latino students were gaining positive affirmation of their identity. I began to recognize that there was so much more that I could be doing.

In examining my curriculum I realized that one art form is never enough to teach the entire history of a people. I am wary of the danger of using only one example, such as the vejigante, to represent all of Puerto Rico's folk arts. I did not want to participate in the practice of exoticizing an art form and culture by limiting students' exposure to the breadth and depth of the arts. The United States has a long, messy history of colonization on the island of Puerto Rico. As an art teacher, I do not want to participate in the "colonization" of any artworks or cultures. This is a complex endeavor.

It would be a gross assumption to presume that every Puerto Rican identifies with the tradition of the vejigante or even knows about it. Puerto Rican students who have lived most of their lives here in the United States have very different experiences from those who have arrived recently from the island. Each community has unique experiences and each family develops its own perspective on those experiences.

Throughout my questioning and critical reflection, I have held steadfast to many aspects of the curriculum that I knew worked well. I have not thrown away my colorful vejigante lesson; rather, I have expanded and built upon it. As my consciousness was raised about the broader context of education through graduate studies and dialogue with Puerto Rican families, I began to include an aspect of the sociopolitical context in each art lesson. In my unit on Puerto Rican art, I now use the vejigante as a starting point to explore many aspects of Puerto Rican life and art. I have developed resources and lessons in three major categories: the earliest Puerto Rican artists, the Taínos; the blending of African, Taíno, Spanish, and other European influences in folk art; and contemporary Puerto Rican artists both on the island and the mainland.

When I began work on this unit, some of my students reminded me: "That's not the Puerto Rico that I know." I responded, "Yes there are so many different communities and experiences in Puerto Rico! Tell me about the Puerto Rico that you know. Let's learn more about that." That is why it is so critical to draw on student knowledge and experience. When using one specific art form, it is essential to place that artwork in its location and history, to emphasize the diversity of the island and the arts it produces. I strive to keep in the foreground that no culture is a monolith, and that no single art form can adequately represent an entire culture. Especially because I am not Puerto Rican, I tell my students, "I am in the process of learning, researching, and exploring, and I need your help." This helps to level the playing field for all students, Puerto Rican or not, to view one another as resources and to draw on the expertise of students and families.

When we discuss race and diversity on the island, we point out the vibrant, resilient heritage of the Puerto Rican community, while simultaneously looking at the hard reality of its marginalization by the United States. The involvement of U.S. business interests in Puerto Rico, which have historically viewed the island as little more than a market for its goods, has wreaked havoc on the environment, language, and livelihood of many

Puerto Ricans throughout the 20th century and to the present. While my students are busily fashioning masks in my art room in Amherst, Massachusetts, I read aloud current front-page news articles about the island of Vieques in Puerto Rico and the debate surrounding the U.S. military presence there. A deeper understanding of the vejigante creates an avenue for understanding the political debates and the different perspectives of the Puerto Rican people surrounding these debates.

In this classroom context, when my students heard about a devastating hurricane in Puerto Rico several years ago, they were motivated to hold bake sales to assist in the relief effort. When they heard about the struggle with the military in Vieques, they were curious to hear more. I use the study of the vejigante mask in my art class to stimulate students' interest in Puerto Rican culture and to heighten their awareness of the politics surrounding Puerto Rico's history. In my struggle to contextualize this art activity, I have found students from all backgrounds in all grade levels hungry to learn more. Parents, caregivers, and community members are eager to share artifacts, stories, and knowledge. This unit will continue to grow as long as my teacher career grows.

I will always remember the day one of my second-grade students, Alejandro, looked up at me and asked, "Ms. Bode, are you Latina—are you Puerto Rican?" I smiled and answered, "No, Alejandro, I am Irish American." He replied, "Why do you love Latino art so much?" "I love it because I learn so much from it, and because there are so many different art forms to study. I love so many kinds of art, but you are right, I sure do love Latino art, especially Puerto Rican art." As an Irish American teacher in a classroom with many diverse youngsters, I make a deliberate effort to practice culturally congruent pedagogy. But expanding the curriculum from a few simple art lessons, and therefore broadening the school culture, did not occur overnight. It is not complete. I now see it as an ongoing process, very much like the growth and education of my students.[9]

Besides thinking and writing about curriculum, another matter of enormous consequence in the intellectual lives of teachers is the question of how they develop expertise. That is, how do teachers learn, or keep learning, about the craft of teaching, about their students, and about their subject matter? According to findings from the National Commission on Teaching and America's Future, what teachers *know* and *do* directly influence what students learn. Moreover, working environments that encourage teachers' continued learning are essential for teacher learning to occur.[10]

Does this imply that effective teachers know all there is to know about their craft? Does it mean that they enter their classrooms sure of themselves and confident of their competence in teaching every day? Surely, this is what one just entering the profession might hope for, and in many ways, it is true that study, experience, and time in the field all contribute to teacher expertise. But teaching is not just a technical activity. While it is in some key ways based on skill and knowledge, teaching is influenced by individual teachers' beliefs, attitudes, values, intuition, and utter uncertainty.

Faith in their abilities as teachers does not mean that teachers are over-confident or smug. Most are not. Many worry about the next lesson, about whether they're doing the best they can, about the choices they're making and whether they're making a difference in the lives of their students. Steve Gordon freely admits that he is *obsessed* with teaching, and this was evident during both our inquiry group meetings and in his writing. Here is part of an E-mail message I received from Steve shortly after one of our meetings:

Is Teaching Rational?

STEPHEN GORDON

Is teaching rational? Can it be? Are there decisions, acts, beliefs that are grounded in truthful, knowledgeable representations of the world encoded in expressible language that compel me and all teachers to be particular teachers/adults with urban, literacy- and politically disenfranchised, usually poor and non-White and non-English-speaking children? I am not looking for prescriptions for teachers. I am not looking for narrow "silver-bullet" programs that script teacher behaviors using some quasi-scientific rationale. It is not the dead-end question of whether teaching is an art or science. I want to find ways to teach that embody the several theories and beliefs that I have come to believe are true and good, truths and knowledge that have consequence for educating urban children. I can do little about the injustice and racism that permeate our institutions.

I want to create pedagogy that makes me feel I have done my best. A recent example approaches what I admire. I work developing student literacy with another teacher, June Robinson (whose basketball coaching duties kept her from being in our inquiry group). Last week we decided after trying to institute literature circle discussions that students had difficulty recognizing and asking a "discussion question." So we backed up to examine how to get students to ask questions and what are different types of questions and what kinds of questions are consequential and worth learning to ask. Through reading we decided on a distinction between "right-there" questions and "inference questions" that Taffy Raphael has written about.[11]

Using a reading from *Fist Stick Knife Gun*, by Geoffrey Canada, that the students are reading, we first trained the leaders of the already formed groups to teach right-there questions to their groups.[12] Then the groups asked the class their questions, the sentence/paragraph of the answer having to be referenced because the answer was "right there" in the text. What was so rewarding for me was that the goal and process of instruction fit my belief in both metacognitive and sociocognitive instruction. Students were teaching one another a method to become more text-aggressive, less paralyzed by text. I believe that many students feel alienated by academic discourse, as if the sentences in texts did not describe the world in which they also lived.

I want students to access, exercise, and express their minds and language, to be able to argue with the assertions and descriptions in their texts. But how do I do that in a way that elicits the language, lived realities, and cognitive processes of my students?

This is hard. What I am reacting against is the narrow "research-based" instructional models that ignore the already existent student language and cognition and discourse, which day-to-day human development in society has generated, in favor of school-based sequential, atomistic, overly prescribed lesson plans. These plans do not arise from the deepest understanding of culture, mind, and language that motivates literacy. It is not that these university-driven programs are completely wrong; rather, they decontextualize learning. They therefore cannot fulfill my ideal of "rational."

What should I do in my class and how should I do it so that my teaching is rational, so that my work arises from and resonates with what I honor as knowledge, what I value in life, and what I want to contribute to my students and profession in this particular society?

As Steve so clearly demonstrated, teaching is not a question of skill and knowledge alone, but a matter of how to take what one has studied and learned and fit it meaningfully into a thousand different contexts, to think about how to connect particular subject matter with specific students in concrete situations that are different from all others. Paulo Freire addressed this issue in a letter to teachers: "An individual's preparation for learning, studying, is before anything else a critical, re-creating activity."[13] All of us know teachers who still use the same lesson plans today that they used 30 years ago. That same worksheet, now yellow with age, has lost not only its color but also its vitality and meaning. But to teach means to *become anew* every day. Those teachers who reinvent themselves and their work every day are the ones who take the challenge to teach seriously. It is a grueling challenge.

When we met again as an inquiry group, Steve read an essay that continued with the same theme as before, that is, his obsession with mindful teaching. He described it as an example of his reflective teaching and said

that he actually wrote it on Sunday night while trying to figure out what
he would do the next day. He went on, "So, there's a personal perspective
of the individual turmoil that accompanies teaching. And then, is there a
way to overcome that turmoil through new perspectives that would sustain one so that even if I get through all this, the other side of it, that I'll
have a hypothesis about what to do?"

In this example of "mindful teaching," Steve Gordon reminds us that
teaching well means getting rid of that worksheet, or at the very least, rethinking its use. Steve was no stranger to teaching. Yet teaching remained
for him a daily challenge, one that defied glib answers or comfortable solutions. It begins with a parody on Edgar Allen Poe's *The Tell-Tale Heart*,
which he changed to have it reflect the teaching context, as a way to suggest the depth of emotion he felt on a Sunday evening as he was preparing
for school the next day.

Obsessed by Mindful Teaching

STEPHEN GORDON

> *"True!—angry, very, very dreadfully angry I had been and am; but why will*
> *you say that I am mad. The 30 years of teaching had sharpened my senses—*
> *not destroyed—nor dulled them. Above all was the sense of injustice and*
> *anomie acute. . . . How, then, am I mad? Hearken! And observe how relent-*
> *lessly I try to tell you my story."*

I have just finished *Fist Stick Knife Gun*, chapters 17–25. With the exception
of 22 and 24, the chapters are about what Geoffrey Canada did to help the
kids of Harlem. What do I want my students to do? As I think this, fear
comes over me. What is its cause? What is it about teaching these ninth
graders that generates such uncertainty and dread? Why do I feel that it is
so hard, that coming up with what is worthwhile is so hard, that being with
them for one hour is so hard? What causes this anxiety? Yes, it is a challenge. Yes, I believe in doing it. In fact, it is my chosen profession, my
decision to do this with students and teachers. But why is it so hard, so
indefinite, so fraught with anxiety as I try to decide what to do, thinking
that Tashia or Crystal or Thomas or . . . will not approve of my decisions, my
work. I think of June and Gail and Denise, my colleagues, as if I am supposed to be able to do something that will affirm I am a good teacher,
appreciated by my students because I have come up with something that
will empower them, that facilitates their learning, that gives them choice to
learn. . . . All of this confuses me. I no longer can be a teacher who blindly
decides what is best for my students. . . . I am trapped by my own psyche

and soul that strives to do the right thing, yet not wanting to work so alone, so hard, and so emotionally in order to do the right thing. I want some certainty, some peace, a feeling which I cannot have.

Do I just live through the anxiety of being a responsible adult who will have to fight for what he believes in, who will have to demand that students do x, y, and z, even as I search for the ways to involve them, engage them, on their own so that the class is theirs, so that literacy grows out of activities that are valued by them and consonant with my deepest values and beliefs?

This piece took my breath away. Many others in the group were equally astonished by Steve's dismay. After all, here was an experienced, confident—and in the judgment of all who knew and had worked with him—exceptionally talented teacher. His anguished thoughts were as touching as they were startling to us. What did Steve's remarks say about teaching and about the impossibility of ever feeling that one is doing enough? This was, What shall I do on Monday morning? writ large. It was, we saw, not simply a question of technique, but one of approach, values, beliefs, faith, even love. What shall I do on Monday morning? in the way that Steve discussed it, became, Am I worthy? Do I know enough to teach? Am I doing a good job?

While Steve Gordon's writing certainly reflected dread, doubt, and uncertainty, it also demonstrated that teaching—good teaching—is never completely mastered. Teaching is ever changing and always interesting and challenging. That one can be moved by teaching to the kind of angst that Steve wrote about indicates, it seemed to us, the existence of a great and bold profession.

Steve Gordon's essay was the impetus for one of the richest conversations in the inquiry group and, therefore, for our continued learning. Perhaps this was so because the uncertainty and perplexity of teaching were so palpable in what he had written. It felt overwhelming, and as a group we wondered if it was possible for a person to do this job consistently, day to day, without being wrong. "I *am* wrong," Steve interrupted, "often." He continued, "I was wrong today." Judith Baker added, "You can kind of see why lots of people don't do this. It's so *painful*."

In the end, Steve Gordon's essay left all of us in the inquiry group feeling more fully human, more hopeful about teaching and ourselves than we had felt when we had started the meeting. Here was a teacher who, having taught for many years, still declared himself uncertain and afraid about what to do the next day ("Forming groups—I know so little about that kind of work," he had said), but who stayed with it for a lifetime.

SUSTAINING COMMUNITY IN TEACHING

What images do prospective teachers have of the craft of teaching? Fed by the popular media, many of them may envision schools as places where individual teachers "make magic" (a phrase Karen Gelzinis used to describe what the best teachers do). But magic does not always happen; sometimes, even the best classrooms are sites of failed attempts to do the right thing. The making of magic and other noble purposes of education require not just individual zeal and effort, but also sustained work in a community. Viewing teachers as members of an intellectual community means understanding that teaching is enriched not only by individual excellence but also by collective effort.

This is not how most new teachers have been taught to think about teaching. Teacher preparation is changing, but new teachers are still commonly treated to a steady diet of incontestable truths, to "best practices," and to methods and formulaic routines to be used in the privacy of their classrooms, as if methods alone were the magic answer to the massive problems that public education faces.[14] How are we to encourage teachers to think otherwise about teaching if this is the prevalent, accepted image of the profession? Who can sustain the kind of energy that individual and private intellectual work entails? How can the profession replenish its ranks with teachers such as Steven Gordon, Judith Baker, Junia Yearwood, and Patty Bode if teaching continues to be seen as a personal endeavor only?

Teachers such as Steven Gordon and others in the What Keeps Teachers Going inquiry group defy the image of teachers as solitary Pied Pipers who take reluctant learners and mysteriously turn them into successful, eager students. As these teachers have found, to be effective, teachers need to learn constantly and in community with others. This means finding colleagues with whom they can talk and argue about and invent, discover, and weave their craft. This is what it means to approach teaching as intellectual work.

Chapter 7

TEACHING AS DEMOCRATIC PRACTICE

With contributions by Stephen Gordon and Mary Cowhey

And as far as making the world, our world, a better place goes, there is no need to distinguish between modest or extravagant actions. Anything that can be done with competence, loyalty, clarity, perseverance, anything that strengthens the fight against the powers of non-love, selfishness, and evil, is equally important.

Paulo Freire, *Teachers as Cultural Workers:*
Letters to Those Who Dare Teach

Teachers enter the profession for any number of reasons, but neither fame nor money nor the promise of lavish working conditions is at the top of that list. Instead, as I have found in my work with teachers over the years, for many of them, social justice figures prominently among the motivating factors underlying their choice to teach. The urge to live a life of service that entails a commitment to the ideals of democracy, fair play, and equality is strong among many of those who begin teaching. Sadly, however, these impulses are sometimes short-lived as the realities of the job become clear. Many who start out with visions of becoming charismatic, heroic teachers in the fashion of romantic Hollywood accounts—both an unrealistic and, ultimately, self-defeating vision—end up crushed and disappointed.

Other factors may explain the longevity of those who continue teaching for the long haul, who remain committed although perhaps not as naive as they once were. Personal history, as we saw in chapter 2, is often at the root of their endurance. For some, their convictions in regard to education have been honed from long years of activism in other just causes. A growing awareness of the unequal treatment received by their students' families and communities explains the commitment of other teachers. They begin to recognize how ideologies of exclusion, in schools and out, unfairly target some students; they begin to react with anger at what Anita Preer, one of the teachers introduced in Chapter 4, called the social problems "that defeat our children."

The injustices that most provoke some teachers' wrath are primarily of two kinds: poverty and its attendant ills; and racism as manifested in society and school. For instance, teachers in the inquiry group spoke repeatedly about the lack of resources in their schools and of the many hardships in their students' lives. Related to poverty, the persistence of racism in schools and society, and the apparent lack of national will to address it, was another reason for the teachers' anger. Many other teachers with whom I've worked share this anger.

In this chapter, I first describe the context of educational injustice in the United States, focusing on the twin evils of poverty and racism. Steve Gordon, a member of the inquiry group, and Mary Cowhey, a first-grade teacher in a school in western Massachusetts, offer eloquent testimony from teachers who are struggling against these injustices while also teaching in a manner that highlights the concept that teaching well means living democracy more fully.

THE STRUGGLE FOR EQUAL EDUCATION

Teachers sometimes rail against the unfairness of a society that makes it eminently clear who the "winners" and "losers" are, and the teachers in the inquiry group are no exception. Rhetoric to the contrary notwithstanding, there is no level playing field for children in our country. This was vividly demonstrated a number of years ago by Jonathan Kozol's groundbreaking exposé of the discrepancies between urban and suburban schools, schools that are sometimes adjacent to one another geographically but, in terms of funding and attention, as different from one another as night is from day.[1] The situation has not changed noticeably since the publication of Kozol's book. Poverty continues to be high in our country: the 20% poverty rate among children in the United States far exceeds levels in other industrialized nations. And poor children are disproportionately represented in our nation's urban schools.

The problems facing students in urban public schools are many, but unfortunately in much of the discussion about these difficulties, the responsibility is placed solely at the feet of the children and their families, as if the problems sprang full blown from them alone. Rather than simply a lack of will or of sound moral character on the part of children, however, the major obstacle in urban schools is the lack of sorely needed resources. Any teacher who works in an urban school system can testify to the truth of this statement. Although money alone can't solve the many problems facing

urban schools, it *can* go a long way toward equalizing the outcomes between children in poorly and well-funded schools. This is because school
funding and academic achievement are related, as shown by a study that
found a strong correlation between level of School funding and rate of child
poverty in terms of eighth-grade mathematics achievement.[2] Consequently,
the discrepancy in support for children of different segments of society is
invariably related to their social class. Race and ethnicity are also implicated in this discussion because Black, Latino, and Native American children are more likely to be poor than are White children; conversely, White
children are more likely to be middle class and enrolled in better-financed
schools than are children of color.

In our country, we tend to scoff at such examples of inequality because
they challenge ideals about fairness that are deeply embedded in our national psyche. Rejecting the reality of inequality, we instead fall back on
arguments of meritocracy, pointing to particular public figures who have
"made it." It is tempting to point to these examples. But when the focus is
only on the personal and familial level, we tend to notice mostly the accomplishments of extraordinary individuals in the face of seemingly
insurmountable odds. It is true that these achievements are admirable, even
heroic. But while achievements of this kind may make us feel good on a
personal level and complacent as a nation, reinforcing the idea that "anyone can make it if she or he works hard enough," concentrating on individual accomplishments does little to alleviate the situation of the great
majority of students in urban schools.

However, if we direct our attention to the *institutional*, *structural* basis
of the dreadful conditions in which poor children are forced to live, we
understand the need for a national commitment to change those conditions.
No child should have to overcome the kinds of odds faced by young people
who live in poverty. It is not simply individual personalities or willpower
that make the difference. In the words of Kathryn Anderson-Levitt, "We
would have to be blind not to notice that, in spite of individuals' strategies
of resistance and thousands of success stories, we can predict with some
regularity which racial and ethnic categories encompass disproportionate
numbers of students failed by the system."[3]

In our nation, access to an equal, high-quality education has long been
regarded as the birthright of all children regardless of station or rank, but
in spite of this cherished ideal, our educational history is replete with examples of grossly uneven access and outcomes. These discrepancies are
more often than not related to students' race/ethnicity, social class, gender, and other differences. Francesco Cordasco, writing more than a quar-
ter of a century ago, described the inequality in U.S. schools this way: "In
a multi-racial, ethnically variegated society, the American experience (cer-

tainly in its schools) has been an experience of cultural assault, discriminatory rejection of educational opportunity for many children, and the continuation of social and economic advantage for a white Anglo-Saxon, Protestant, middle-class patrician elite."[4] Once the civil rights movement began in earnest, public education was the focus of much of its agenda. The struggle has not been easy, because public education has represented both the high ideals of equality and the limited vested interests that challenge those high ideals. The resulting tension has been critically evident in the area of race. According to educational historian David Tyack, "Attempts to preserve white supremacy and to achieve racial justice have fueled the politics of education for more than a century."[5]

Even recent reforms, however, have not changed the situation in any appreciable way. In a report of 16 schools around the country engaged in middle-school reforms through the massive Turning Points initiative, researchers found that the reforms did little to interrupt "the course of the nation's history, flaws, and inequity, its hegemony and racism."[6] Rather than being a paragon of educational equality, in the recent past, U.S. schools have consistently ranked among the most unequal in the industrialized world in terms of spending, curricular offerings, and teaching quality.[7] Schools are not an aberration in an otherwise just society that is characterized by fair play and equality. In spite of our society's passionate ideology of equality, as a nation we have a long way to go in reaching this goal.

Public education in the United States thus presents a complex and conflicted picture of extraordinary opportunities for some and restricted access for others. Although in our society education has been understood as a major gateway out of poverty—and it has served this function admirably for some—academic success has been elusive for large numbers of young people who are economically disadvantaged or culturally and racially different from the "mainstream," or both. In a penetrating statement that says as much about our schools as it does about our society, after a national tour of high schools a number of years ago, Ted Sizer wrote, "It got so I could say with some justification to school principals, 'Tell me about the incomes of your students' families and I'll describe to you your school.'"[8] Something is terribly wrong.

RACISM IN SCHOOLS AND SOCIETY

Racism, ubiquitous as it is in society, also finds its way into schools. It is common to think of racism simply as name-calling or as acts of vandalism or violence. But it is not only through racial slurs and teasing that racism is apparent. While it is true that most schools in our society have come a long way because they take a firm stand against such behaviors, racism and other biases comprise more than just obvious behaviors such as these. While racism may be manifested as individual acts of small-mindedness, such as a preference on the part of teachers for some children over others, even more insidious and damaging than personal acts of bigotry or small-mindedness is *institutional racism*. Institutional racism is most clearly demonstrated through particular policies and practices that grant privilege to some people over others simply because of their race.

Institutional racism is commonly embedded in school policies and practices in ways that may appear natural and normal. This includes tracking, in which majority-group children are invariably overrepresented in high-ability tracks and other children end up in low-ability tracks, especially in the sciences and math; curriculum that effectively negates or denies the presence of others besides the majority in history, the arts, or any other endeavors; or even in letters sent home in English to families that do not speak or understand it. Such practices may appear to be fair and "color-blind" because, after all, they treat all children the same. But as Evelyn Hanssen, a White teacher who developed a growing awareness of institutional racism and how it is manifested in schools explains, "We need to remember that institutional racism typically isn't ugly. Rather than being expressed through racial slurs, it tends to be wrapped in noble proclamations of tradition, fairness, and high standards. Rather than being a rare incident, it is woven into the fabric of our historically racist society."[9]

An example from the inquiry group comes from Ambrizeth Lima, a bilingual teacher who thought often about racism and alienation. She explained that one of the primary reasons she had become a teacher was to protect Cape Verdean students from the kind of treatment she had experienced as an immigrant. The *personal* attacks her students encountered were worrying enough, but she was even more concerned about *institutional* arrangements in schools, arrangements that tended to reinforce societal biases against particular students. In the bilingual program, this included segregation of bilingual students from others in the school and subtle but tangible barriers to their participation in school-related activities outside the bilingual program.

Ambrizeth had written movingly about her experience when she arrived in the United States and was placed in a bilingual program. In a chapter she wrote for a book on bilingual education, she described the bilingual program as an oasis within an otherwise alienating institution. She had reflected on what it was like to be deprived of her language and culture as a new immigrant in the larger setting: "A part of me died in my new school. I became mute—or perhaps people around me became deaf. I became invisible, or maybe people lost their sight."[10]

Ambrizeth saw a similar thing happening with the Cape Verdean students she was teaching. They resisted speaking Cape Verdean Crioulo or Portuguese (some spoke both), and they felt ashamed of their identity. She was certain that these behaviors developed as a result of the perceptions of teachers, even well-intentioned teachers, about their students' identities. At an inquiry group meeting, she had explained: "I think the major difference is in the attitude toward what a student is when they first get here, what they have, whether we will look at it as something valuable and take from what that kid is bringing and use it or if we try to erase it and just set the kid up with some vocabulary words in English."

They may not have entered the teaching profession with this goal in mind, but in their everyday work, teachers who work in urban schools inevitably end up struggling against racism and other injustices. There is no blueprint for doing so. Whether through their lesson plans or the strategies they select or by speaking up at teachers' meetings or suggesting changes in school policies, teachers' work is often about educational justice.

TEACHING AS EDUCATIONAL JUSTICE

Near the end of our time together, I suggested that inquiry group members read and discuss Paulo Freire's *Teachers as Cultural Workers: Letters to Those Who Dare Teach*.[11] The book, written for teachers in Brazil and published after Freire's death, consists of a series of 10 letters to teachers focusing on the profession of teaching and on the larger purposes of education. In it, Freire also addresses specific issues of pedagogy, language, culture, and literacy.

I thought it would be useful for inquiry group members to discuss some of Freire's ideas. Although Freire wrote to teachers in a context far different from that of urban schools in the United States, we found many significant insights and even parallels between the two situations. We had fruitful and thought-provoking discussions about the book, and it seemed to stir us all to think more deeply about teaching and the role of teachers. Consequently, I asked them to write a letter to a new teacher in the style of the Freire book and of the book by Vito Perrone, *A Letter to Teachers: Reflections on Schooling and the Art of Teaching*, with which some of them were also familiar.[12] Given their experiences and insights, I was curious to know what they would say to new teachers.

In their letters, a number of the teachers expressed pride in the mission of their work and dismay at how they were treated. They shared the lessons they had learned along the way with new teachers, and they reflected on what it means to be a teacher today in a struggling urban school.

Many spoke about teaching as educational justice. Steve Gordon's letter is a good example.

Letter to a New Teacher

STEPHEN GORDON

Dear Colleague,

You have made your decision. Against the advice of relatives and friends who counseled you against this career path, you have decided to teach. Reasons beyond starting salary and perceived prestige have called you to become a teacher, fully aware of how little gratitude and respect teachers receive in our free-enterprise society that values wealth over justice.

You have concluded that being an adult responsible for the education of children is your calling. Why is that? What do you hope to give and receive as a teacher? When you see yourself in a classroom working with other people's children, what do you see yourself doing and saying that is so necessary to you—and them? Why do you want to teach? Why this school? Why these particular children? I suggest you write the answers to these questions now; examine and discuss them with those who care about your happiness. I hope that your answers motivate and sustain you in your day-to-day struggle to make a difference in the lives of your students. I hope the answers give you the courage and self-knowledge to endure and succeed—and to find allies in your work.

I welcome you into my chosen profession. Beginning on your first day of teaching and perhaps never leaving, anxiety and self-doubt may be your constant shadow. They have been for me. I have felt isolated and ineffective, even abandoned by colleagues and administrators. I see and feel the realities of my students, their wants and needs, and I think I have failed them, that I have not done the right thing, or enough. And I have become angry, ascribing my students' failure to racial and economic injustice.

I have learned to accept, even welcome, this dread, guilt, and anger. These emotions, I believe, have kept me honest, a spur to understanding what I must do and a shield against facile, mindless, so-called solutions that repeatedly surface in a culture that refuses to recognize complexity and confront injustice. Rather than give you advice, let me share with you how I have attempted to sustain my commitment to my students, colleagues, and students after 30 years of teaching high school in Boston.

I have learned to acknowledge and express the anger that arises from the wide discrepancy between my goals for my students and their current achievement. I ascribe this disparity to the failure of our system to do educational justice for my students. I have seen students whose power and will to learn seem to have atrophied, students who do not possess the motivation and self-discipline necessary to excel, students who seem conditioned to compliance or resistance. I interpret these student attitudes and behaviors as the result of low expectations, misguided pedagogy, and spurious systemwide "solutions"—including the current standards and high-stakes-testing movements. Nevertheless, I continue to hold my students personally responsible for their performance.

No matter how emotionally seductive and satisfying, I have consciously sought to avoid generalizations and accusations that might mitigate my disappointment at the expense of my students—their language, their parents, their race and culture. I acknowledge my frustration and do not repress my anger. By expressing my anger I am forced to examine my students' learning needs and my teaching practices. By so doing, I am affirming hope and the willingness to take responsibility for my students' success.

I try to express my hopes and disappointments to my students, telling them what I expect and want from them. I believe that my expressed expectations will help teach them to take more responsibility for their own education, so that they will not merely comply or resist. I frequently ask them to evaluate the educational validity of what and how I am teaching. They must participate in their own education—a respectful fit between their individual cognitive and linguistic development and the school's academic requirements must be found. I have not yet succeeded in creating such a classroom community that counteracts years of negative school culture, but I will continue trying. This has been hard for me because I do not yet know how to engender sufficient student self-discipline and self-determination. Maybe you can help me. I have much more to learn.

To survive and grow, I had to find colleagues who share my anger, hopes, beliefs, and assumptions about students and teaching. When I discuss my teaching with these caring colleagues, I work to specify exactly what troubles me; I fight the fear that having problems means I am doing something wrong. By example, I seek to help my colleagues to become more professionally vulnerable, to name the individual classroom realities that inhibit their success and threaten their self-image as competent professionals. I avoid solving colleagues' problems by giving them advice; instead, through questioning, I work to find a way for them to reveal exactly what is troubling and why. Sharing difficult truths and emotions has been necessary for my personal and professional development. Fortunately, I have been a member of several teacher-research and inquiry groups that have supported this honesty, helping me to examine and improve my teaching.

However, these truths and emotions have been necessary but not sufficient to endure. I have learned to turn what troubles me about my students and/or my classroom into a researchable question. This may be difficult at first, for I have had to cultivate an inquiry stance about my teaching practice. I have learned to do research about my troubling questions, finding and reading what fellow teachers and researchers have discovered. For example, as an English teacher I joined the National Council of Teachers of English and the International Reading Association. I read their professional journals. I want to create an intellectual community in my school wherein teachers share and discuss articles and books. I have become a teacher because I believe in intellectual development. I must take care of my own. I have found inspiring, supportive, and insightful authors who have taught me and affirmed my perspective. I think of Paulo Freire, Lev Vygotsky, Lisa Delpit, and James Gee. And I would not be writing this letter had it not been for Sonia Nieto.

I am happy that I found a profession that combines my belief in social justice with my zeal for intellectual excellence. My career choice has meant much anxiety, anger, and disappointment. But it has also produced profound joy. I have spent my work life committed to a just cause: the education of Boston high school students. Welcome to our noble teaching profession and our enduring cause.

With hope and faith,
Stephen Gordon

TEACHING FOR DEMOCRACY

In the United States, we pride ourselves on living in a democracy, yet we afford our young people precious few experiences in preparation for it. Every election day, we bemoan the fact that fewer than half of those eligible to vote do so. But why should this surprise us? We give lip service to preparing students for active membership in a democratic society, but we rarely provide the possibility for an apprenticeship in democracy in schools, because our pedagogy and curriculum are often at odds with this mission. The curriculum, for instance, pays scant attention to the undemocratic, exclusionary, ugly side of history that is just as much a part of our collective heritage as is the democratic, inclusive, noble side. Not only is the process of democracy missing, so is the critical content of democracy that would expose all students to its contradictory dimensions. In many schools, we find democratic practices only in textbooks, and these are often confined to idealistic discussions of the American Revolution. In the meantime, most students have little chance to practice day-to-day democracy, with all its messiness and conflicts. Students can see these contradictions clearly in their own lives, so to completely ignore them in their schooling sends a message that only half-truths can be taught. These problems affect us all, not only teachers and students.

To teach for democracy can mean many things. It can mean teaching students a fuller, more complicated history; it can mean being more inclusive, making certain that silenced voices are included in the telling; it can mean building a democratic environment for learning; it can mean questioning stereotypes and labels; and it can mean teaching children, even the youngest among them, to question what they are learning. After all, progress has usually been made not by those who go along but by those who challenge the rules, whether we are speaking of the American Revolution or the civil rights movement.[13] One teacher who does all these things is Mary Cowhey, a magnificent teacher and also a former student of mine. Just as I was completing work on the manuscript for this book, I thought to ask Mary to share her thoughts about what keeps teachers going. Her response came quickly. The E-mail message she sent me stresses democratic teaching and educational justice, both for individual students and for learning to live in community.

Mary is a loving, devoted teacher. Above all, she wants the students she teaches (first graders this year, but in the past she has taught both first and second graders) to learn to think critically and act morally, to be creative and serious thinkers, and to understand the power that they have, individually and collectively, to change the world. Every day in her classroom is an adventure, as you will see below. No matter when you ask, Mary has an inspiring story to tell about something that happened with her students that same day. Mary wants students to challenge authority, even hers; she teaches them to always ask, Where's the evidence? And so, every time she teaches them something new, her students ask, "Where's the evidence?!"

Mary Cowhey loves teaching. She came into it later than most teachers, in her mid-30s. She had been a community organizer for many years, working primarily with African American and Latino communities and learning Spanish along the way. Then she decided to change careers. I was curious to know why she had done so, and why she remained in teaching. Although she does not teach in an urban school, the small city in which she teaches is enormously diverse in terms of social class, race, ethnicity, native language, and family structure, and it is beset by some of the same challenges and problems as those found in urban schools. Her response to me is as thorough and thoughtful a justification for teaching democratically as I have seen anywhere.

A Way to Live in the World

MARY COWHEY

Dear Sonia,

It is so wonderful to hear from you. I am glad your book is coming along, that you've had a chance to focus on it this month. I would love to give you something for your book. I am sorry for all the times I've been slow to respond to your invitations and suggestions, so this time I will not write it on a list. I will just write you this letter. Since I do not know how to save things on E-mail, I will just have to finish it and send it before Mairead gets up from her nap.

Teaching is a way to live in the world. I just can't see myself living in this world if I am not doing something positive. Size and effectiveness do not matter too much to me, if I nurture one plant or a large garden, if I help one person well, if I reach 20 children and their families in a year, or thousands, what is important is that I do it and do it well, that I do it with heart. The process of teaching, of organizing, of caring, of nurturing—I believe it makes me a better person. I don't mean better than the next person. I mean a better person than I was yesterday. Clearly the better part is debatable. Better or not, it makes me a person, makes me human, makes me think and learn, makes me alive.

I was not always with people. Once I was a hermit, you know. I lived in a small tent in the woods and ate rice and beans and granola and wild strawberries while they lasted. I learned many things, about the woods and about myself. Of course I was learning then, but I wasn't teaching. I made a point of surviving, but I ask myself now, how was I living? Perhaps in my youth, I was thinking that by living quietly, gently, owning and using very little, I was somehow helping the planet. That was more than 20 years ago, and that was the last time I ever lived and worked alone like that. I came to realize that it wasn't all about seeing how little one can take or use (although I don't think that's a bad idea and still try to live simply) but rather how one gives. I am not talking about great deeds and award-winning accomplishments, just the giving and caring that comes from human connections, living in community, turning toward and not away when there is a need. I guess that would be a generosity of spirit.

I organized for 14 years, because I wanted to change the world. I fought evictions and unfair firings, utility cutoffs and condemnations. I fought to get people their food stamps and I fought to get people into drug rehab centers. I taught English and labor history and workers' rights. I organized pickets and meetings and made speeches and wrote articles and leaflets. I organized truckloads of food, clothes, blankets, and firewood. I fought and I worked until I was nearly gone. I stopped when it seemed my soul was all used up, when I had grown dry inside, when I no longer felt human.

When I began to teach, I embraced Paulo Freire's idea that teaching is political. I took a very deep breath and told myself that if I could touch 18 children and their families in a year that would change the world a little. If I could keep one child from losing hope, that would help the world a little. If students left my class a little more open minded, less biased, thinking critically, with even a little experience of using their reading, writing, and math skills as tools for justice and social change, healing or helping, that would change the world some.

I use children's literature to teach first graders the fundamentals of activism before diving straight into civil rights history, to help develop a schema for cooperation, protest, demand, negotiation, strikes, and boycotts. I just read this book, *Click, Clack, Moo: Cows That Type*, about cows who find an old typewriter in the barn and type letters to the farmer, demanding electric blankets.[14] When the farmer refuses, they go on strike and refuse to give milk. Next they type a letter saying the hens want electric blankets. When the farmer refuses them all, the hens join the strike and refuse to lay eggs. After the read-aloud and discussion, I mentioned to my new student teacher that you have to be a little careful when you introduce ideas like this to your students.

Later, I joined a table of boys at snack time. After I sat down, I realized they had been talking excitedly among themselves about the idea of students striking to play instead of attending school. David, a loud, lively boy, asked me, "Would that work? Can kids strike?" I thought about it, and then told them about how under apartheid the students of Soweto in South Africa had basically struck, refusing to attend classes and demonstrating, to protest having to learn Afrikaans, the language of their white oppressors.

Curtis looked over at the photographs of our pen pals at several schools in South Africa. He said to David, "I think our pen pals would think we are crazy. They have to pay money to go to a school with hardly any books and no toilet, and we get to go to school for free." John said, "I think kids in Afghanistan really want to go to school too, and they don't have any." Another boy agreed, and David said that more playtime wouldn't be a good reason for students to strike. Allan, a very shy, thoughtful boy, had been sitting quietly during this lively exchange. When he spoke, it was little more than a whisper to his cracker, "We could do it to stop the war." David said to him loudly, "What do you mean, stop the war?" Very softly, still without making eye contact, Allan said, "Maybe kids could go on strike to stop the war in Afghanistan."

Sometimes they take my breath away.

Day to day, I don't always know what will be the thing that works. Sometimes I don't learn about it until later. One day I called the mother of a very troubled little boy to let her know how well her son was doing in reading. She was a little quiet. Then she said, "You know, you are the first person who ever called to tell me anything good about my son."

I am thinking of your title/idea, what keeps teachers going in spite of everything. One thing that strikes me as I write this is the importance of the relationships with parents, with families. (By parents I mean all of their loving adults and caregivers). Children are such a mystery. I am a parent and a teacher. Parents don't usually get to see their children in the school, and the teachers don't usually get to see them in the family. I know that what I observe in school is a fraction of what they understand and have learned. Likewise, progress reports three times each year and two conferences let the parents see even a smaller fraction of that. From the start of each school year, even before the school doors open, I work to build that relationship with families. Whether it is done by home visits or arranging some unhurried conversations with families early in the year, that foundation is vital. Writing a weekly newsletter to the families about what we've done and what we will be doing next gives the families some context for understanding the child's assignments, questions, and observations. It builds enthusiasm for our work and reinforces it at home. I love talking to family members as they drop off and pick up the children. I care about these families.

What else keeps me going in spite of everything? My principal. I have the most wonderful principal in the world. I wouldn't want her job for anything in the world, but I thank God (and her) every day that she does it. She creates a climate in our school that allows me to teach and grow the way I do. She loves every child in the school and is passionate about peace, equity, global culture, and other things I care about, and she loves to join us whenever we invite her. Other teachers keep me going, like my husband, Bill; like Kim Gerould next door; like the new first-grade teacher down the hall that I mentor; like the student teacher I had last semester; like the teachers I met in South Africa when I went to the United Nations World Conference Against Racism last summer. Even as another's teacher's struggles are different from mine, I learn by listening and watching and helping. Again it is the process that keeps me going, that we share a passion to do this amazing thing called teaching well. There is a camaraderie in that.

Intellectual work—of course there is that. Sometimes I wish, just for a moment or an hour, that I could stop thinking, or at least stop thinking of new things. Really though, I would die. Though I often drive myself crazy by thinking too much, it keeps me going. New ideas, new questions to find answers to, new people to ask and find out, new problems to solve, new angles to see things from, motivation to do something that I might not have been passionate about before. Here's a little example. I used to think, Why teach magnets to first graders or simple machines to second graders, aside from the fact that the state curriculum frameworks say so? Really, what does the average college-educated professional or tradesperson (not electricians) know about magnets? That they have poles, that opposites attract and likes repel, that magnetism has something to do with how compasses and electricity work. Really, most of us don't mind knowing very little about it. Why should a 6-year-old care? Should I just give them magnets to play with, call it a "science center," say I've "covered magnetism," and move along? It bugged me that there must be a reason that I was missing.

Last year I decided to take a seminar in physics. It was such a terrible experience that it was good. First of all, I felt like a second-language learner all over again. The professors, who said the course required no background in math or science, were teaching it to the level of high school physics teachers. I was the only elementary teacher there; I don't know why all those high school physics teachers signed up. I thought they already *knew* physics. I was so angry and frustrated that I cried the first day. I didn't know all the words and symbols the other people were using. I got so angry trying to prove my point to some other science teachers in my group that I took off my shoe and hooked it to a scale to make my point. I fought my way through the whole course, telling myself, "I am not stupid!" solving the problems by clawing my way through them with completely unorthodox, often primitive methods that sometimes worked or were often at least on the right track. When I taught a second-grade science unit on simple machines (another unit I previously didn't understand the point of) after that, I was hot! I used *The Way Things Work* and thought, Why didn't those stupid professors use this book?[15] I was excited intellectually and the kids felt it. At our class picnic at the end of the year, I could hear the kids playing on the playground. "I'm going down the inclined plane!" "Want to come on the lever with me? Scoot closer to the fulcrum 'cause you're bigger!" When I learned more about it, I could make it matter.

Children. I teach my students like I want my children taught. I want them challenged and loved. When I see my own children and other children, in my school or in a South African school, they keep me going. They need good teaching, the best. That drives me on.

Good teachers. I often think of teachers who really loved their subject or who really loved me or listened to me or encouraged me or took me seriously or pushed me to do my best work. You are one of those teachers in my life. Rita Rappoport, my seventh-grade English teacher, who read my journal and always wrote back. My ninth-grade teacher, Terry Rowan, took my poetry seriously and invited me to join his poetry workshop. They keep me going, even though I may never see them again. I feel like I owe them. After all that work and love they put into me, I ought to be damn good. I ought to pass it on.

OK, Sonia—Robeson and Bill are home from the library. I've let the fire burn down to embers in the stove. Friends are coming for dinner in 20 minutes and I haven't started cooking. Mairead has been reading books to dolls in her crib for an hour. I'm terrible. But I've enjoyed this. It feels like talking with you. Writing, like talking, helps me think, reflect. I hope some little bit of this might be useful to you. Use it however you would like.

Peace,
Mary

FINDING EQUILIBRIUM

Viewing teaching as educational justice presents both opportunities and dilemmas. Teachers, especially those in urban schools, understand too well that teaching today is vastly different from what it was 100 or 50 or even 20 years ago. They realize that they must attend to a host of problems that might have seemed inconceivable then, problems related to poverty, hopelessness, and injustice of all kinds. They cannot ignore these problems, yet they also cannot single-handedly solve them. Even if they could, that is not the role of teachers.

Teachers are not miracle workers. Nor are they social workers or missionaries, and viewing teaching as educational justice can sometimes produce a missionary mentality among educators. This mentality is not helpful to students or to their parents or to members of their communities, who may resent it. Becoming the Holden Caulfield of the classroom, saving children from the hardships they endure, is neither possible nor the answer to their problems. Teachers need to understand their role as involving more than simply attending to the minds of students; it also entails nurturing their hearts and souls. But to do this without taking on the world of injustice is tricky business.

Ambrizeth Lima, Steve Gordon, and Mary Cowhey understand this tension. For me, their teaching practices represent heroic ways of reaching the right balance—an equilibrium that is difficult at best. No wonder, then, that even among committed teachers—those who remain working for many years and sometimes in the most difficult circumstances—teaching is extraordinarily trying. And yet they continue. What is their "secret"? The secret of being an effective teacher, and of having the stamina to continue, was a recurring theme in inquiry group discussions. It is an issue to which we turn in the following chapter.

Chapter 8

TEACHING AS SHAPING FUTURES

With contributions from Karen Gelzinis and Junia Yearwood

If you don't know a student, there's no way to influence him. If you don't know his background, there's no way you are going to get in touch with him. There's no way you're going to influence him if you don't know where he's been.

Manuel Gomes, in Sonia Nieto, *Affirming Diversity: The Sociopolitical Context of Multicultural Education*

These words of Manuel Gomes, a student who was interviewed by Carol Shea a number of years ago for a book I was writing about students of diverse backgrounds, are especially poignant because Manuel didn't feel that many teachers had tried to know "where he's been" in any but the most superficial way. In the end, it was a theater workshop in the school that helped him with some of the issues he was facing daily as a new immigrant to this country and as a new student in his school: adjusting to a new society, learning a new language, struggling with his identity, "fitting in," coping with his father's life-threatening illness, and living in poverty. Attempts to learn about their students was at the heart of the work I did with the inquiry group teachers, but it is evident that this concern is not present in all teachers.

Although most teachers are sincere in their efforts to reach all students, some never do. In fact, many teachers do not know very much about the students they teach, for many reasons. For one, teachers' experiences and identities are often quite different from those of their students. Given the changing demographics of schools, these differences are more obvious now than ever: Black, Asian, American Indian, and Latino students now account for nearly 39% of students in U.S. public schools, while teachers are overwhelmingly White (almost 90%).[1] In their professional education, most teachers have had little preparation for teaching students who are different from them. Although schools of education and in-service professional development courses are evolving to reflect the nation's demographic changes, it is still too often the case that teachers are at a loss to understand students who differ from them in race/ethnicity, culture, social class, and native language.

Demographics by themselves, however, are not the only reason that teachers and their students find it difficult to communicate. The very structure of schools makes communication and relationship building difficult, and this is especially true in urban high schools. Many high schools are hectic places, and the bigger they are the more hectic life seems to be; since most urban high schools are large, students may experience them as unfriendly and distant spaces. In many high schools, teachers and students alike are in a constant hustle from class to class, meeting to meeting, and crisis to crisis. Large schools also tend to be impersonal places. Teachers may see up to 150 students each day, making it a near certainty that they never really get to know any of them. Given this situation, the desire to create smaller schools is understandable. Small schools may alleviate some of the problems of larger schools, but size is also not the only problem.[2] Rather, a constellation of reasons helps explain why it is so difficult for teachers and students to get to know one another.

It became clear to us in the inquiry group that building relationships is crucial for *both* student achievement *and* teacher retention. In the words of Karen Gelzinis in this chapter, *teachers change lives forever*. The impact that teachers may have on students' lives makes it even more imperative that teachers choose their words carefully. But given the pace of their days, teachers rarely have the time to choose each word they say with the precision of, say, writers, or even of university professors. Yet teachers' words are probably more consequential than those spoken by members of almost any other profession, and the words of their classmates can affect students' lives. In one report about immigrant students in California, almost every student interviewed said that they had at one time or another been spat upon, tricked, teased, or laughed at because of their race or accent or because of the way they dressed; most could also cite instances in which they were punished, publicly embarrassed, or made fun of *by their teachers* because of these students' improper use of English.[3]

What teachers do and say may stay with their students for a lifetime. That is the major message of this chapter, which includes pieces written by Junia Yearwood, who teaches English and African American history, and Karen Gelzinis, a math teacher and Junia's colleague at the same school.

In thinking about the major issue she wanted to explore for her work in the inquiry group, Junia Yearwood settled on the question of the impact of teachers' words on the lives of students. Junia had thought about this issue for many years, as you'll see at the beginning of her essay. She asked students to help her out with this question. What she found through her research strikingly demonstrates how words (and the attitudes behind them) have the ability to either inspire or dampen students' enthusiasm for school and learning.

The Power of Their Words

JUNIA YEARWOOD

Memories of my grandmother calling me a wretch are imprinted on the panels of my mind. In the 5th decade of my life, these memories have a way of spontaneously resurfacing. They are accompanied by the intense, negative physical and emotional reactions I experienced the first time the word was hurled in my direction: My body cringes and my spirit recoils. How I hated that word!

In her article "Words That Kill," Edith Fraser accurately describes my personal experience: "Every day thousands of children are hammered with cruel words of sarcasm and ridicule. Their minds are seared not by cigarettes, but by painful statements that can be played on the tape recorder of their brain, to be rewound and played again and again."[4] Emotional abuse is the subject she is addressing. When we use derogatory terms with children, we are putting them down, and this is an example of emotional abuse. I began to wonder how many times I had inadvertently done this to my students. How many times have I witnessed the devastation that emotional abuse leaves in its wake in the corridors of the schools in which I have taught? Probably too many and too often.

This revelation became the impetus for my line of inquiry. What do we say to our students? Do our words, positive or negative, affect them? What do our gestures and actions say? Do the things we say affect our students' academic performance and their sense of self? The members of the inquiry group at my high school unanimously agreed that the answers to my queries lay in our students and that the best means of discovery was a student survey. With the help of my colleagues, I eventually devised a group of questions I hoped would give some insight or uncover some answers to my burning question.

Words That Kill

One of the important pieces of information provided by the survey is that students listen to what we say. They not only listen intently, but they remember our words, especially when those words and the feelings they summon persist for many years. A number of my ninth graders recalled statements and incidents they experienced or witnessed in first grade and even kindergarten. I will never forget the intensity and visible anger on the face of one 12th grader as he recounted an incident that occurred in fifth grade in which he believed a teacher had treated him unfairly. In response to one of the questions on the survey, another student who had graduated and was already a sophomore in college wrote, "Too hard to talk about."

Our students carefully observe and monitor our words, gestures, facial expressions, and actions. We never know when we are creating memories—memories of shame and embarrassment or recollections of pride, hope, and validation. As one of my colleagues, Roberta Logan, a veteran social studies teacher, so wisely stated, "Our students may not be able to read the textbook, but they can sure read you." I am yet to read an autobiography in which a memory of a particular teacher is not recounted because of either its positive effect on the author's life or its legacy of humiliation, anger, or pain.

No child should ever have to say, "I never learned hate at home, or shame. I had to go to school for that. I was 7 years old when I got my first big lesson." These ominous words are those of Dick Gregory, referring to the day he was verbally chastised and destroyed by his teacher in the presence of his classmates, in his autobiography, *Nigger*.[5] Such examples of verbal and emotional abuse are not anomalies in the classrooms of the students who responded to my survey. In many cases these incidents seem to be the norm. There was no dearth of examples of experiences of degradation offered by my students. They said that teachers called them, among many other words, *stupid, slow, ignorant, fat, dumb, punk.* They said that teachers made comments such as "You'll never amount to anything," "Shut up," "You can't even pass a test," "Even if you study, you'll still fail," "That was a dumb answer," and "You are the worst student." One said that when he failed a test, the teacher said, "I'm not surprised," and another volunteered that his fourth-grade teacher had said, "I should put you in kindergarten." Another student said a teacher had told him that in a couple of years, he would be either dead or in jail.

Our students are sometimes rude and they press us to the limit. They are experts at observing and identifying our weaknesses and pushing our anger buttons. However, our sense of frustration, ire, and in some instances hopelessness should never become an excuse for losing control over our words and actions. We would never tolerate our physician losing control and publicly belittling us no matter how frustrated he or she may be with our noncompliance with his or her orders or with our slow medical progress. We would be outraged if our dentist yelled or muttered words of ridicule as we sat muzzled in the chair. We expect doctors, dentists, lawyers, and all other professionals to be just that, professionals. We too are professionals; our profession is a noble one and our students expect and deserve to be the beneficiaries of the proficiency, skill, and respect that our profession demands. Self-discipline is the key. As teachers, we must practice what we strive to impart to our students—not only academic skills, but also the skill of choosing words carefully and wisely.

Words That Build

In his book *Lives on the Boundary*, Mike Rose describes teaching as "a kind of romance."[6] Teaching as a kind of romance, the teacher the wooer: giving a pat on the back, offering conversation. Intriguing and novel imagery of what we do. Love for our students is one major impetus for keeping our passion for teaching alive. The ways in which we demonstrate our love and how our students respond to these demonstrations are pivotal in our effectiveness.

In my survey, I asked students what teachers did or said to show that they believed students were smart. Students wrote that teachers smiled, talked to them, gave them a pat on the back, looked proud of them, or "pulled me to the side and told me that I was doing good." Students gave the following reasons for thinking that what a teacher thinks or believes about them affects how they feel about themselves:

"Yes, because if he or she tells me I'm smart, I will feel happy and start doing my work."
"If a teacher believes in you, it gives the student more confidence about himself or herself."
"I think if a teacher does not believe in me, I WILL NEVER AMOUNT TO ANYTHING."

Mike Rose's enthusiasm for writing was driven by his desire to be liked, and Maya Angelou broke out of her self-imposed silence and began her fascination with poetry because, in her words, "I was liked, and what a difference it made. . . . I didn't question why Mrs. Flowers [her neighborhood, informal "teacher"] had singled me out for attention. All I cared about was that she made cookies for me and read to me from her favorite book."[7]

Words, beliefs, actions: Sometimes teachers do not realize the tremendous impact these can have. The reaction of Junia's students to her survey is certainly an indication of this. But even more than being simply hurtful or complimentary, teachers' words and beliefs can also shape futures.

Karen Gelzinis thought about this matter a great deal. She sent me the writing piece that follows shortly before the beginning of the 2000 school year and 4 months after the last meeting of the inquiry group. For that final meeting, we had gathered at a beautiful, secluded retreat outside Boston, an idyllic spot that could not have been more different from the noisy, crowded urban schools where the inquiry group teachers worked. On her way to the meeting, Karen had picked up two cards, one for me and the other for Ceronne Daly, who had helped organize our monthly meetings. The cards said simply, "Teachers Change Lives Forever."

We spent an enchanted day together, talking, writing, eating, even shedding a few tears. It was the end of our inquiry into *What keeps teachers going in spite of everything?* and although we hadn't come up with the "secret," we knew we were on to something. At the end of the meeting, I asked the teachers to send me their writing. I knew I wanted to share our work with many people; it was too valuable to remain in just the heads and hearts of a small group of dedicated teachers in Boston. Karen didn't get around to sending me anything until mid-August. Her mind was too full of school, of students, of rubrics and benchmarks and "best practices" to find the time to write. But when she finally was able to do it—on August 11, the day that summer school finished—it was an outpouring of many of the motivations, frustrations, and joys of teaching she had been thinking about for a long time. In the letter, she wrote extensively about the questions about teaching that tear at her soul; about her students; and about Sonie Felix, her former student and now also a teacher in the Boston public schools, who was going through her own crisis in teaching. What follows is just a part of the long letter she sent me.

Teachers Change Lives Forever

KAREN GELZINIS

Dear Sonia,

Summer school ended yesterday. For me and for many of my students, it was the first time that we had ever had to go to summer school (This is what I hate about putting things down on paper . . . I see a little word like "had" and my mind starts going again. *I* did not have to go, I made the choice. And yet, I didn't really have a choice because these were *my* kids. This year, a special transition summer school was put together for kids in "transition" years—having to do with state testing. If you taught this summer school program, you could have the kids that you taught during the year. If I didn't teach them, who would they have had? Teachers were even hired from other school systems for this program, you didn't even have to be a teacher of the subject that you taught during the summer).

You can see why I don't like to write. I've also been living with the fact that I haven't sent you anything. But believe me, it has not been out of my mind.

Our retreat at the mansion was a special day. That night, I had all kinds of thoughts, and even some answers, I felt, running through my head. This was it. I *knew* that I would put it all down during the coming weekend and get it off to you. But, again, the more I thought, the more I thought. . . . And now it is August 11th.

I do want you to know, however, how important the whole year has been to me (and as I finished those last couple of words, I want you to know that the tears started again. Perhaps this is why I don't like to write).

I could never understand when people with whom I taught, and people who I knew were good teachers, would say that they couldn't see themselves doing this for another 10, 15 years. Until a few years ago, I always felt that I could easily be one of those women who would be 70 years old and still appearing each September. But I sensed a change in myself in the past few years, and I knew it wasn't because of the kids (and again I feel the tears, but you have to know that I still cry whenever I watch *The Wizard of Oz*, and Dorothy asks, "Toto, too?" and the good witch replies, "Toto too"). No, it was definitely not the kids. Could they drive me crazy? Yes. But it wasn't the kids. Had something changed in me? I really didn't think so, because my happiest times were when I was in my class-room with my kids. It's all the other *stuff*: the constant talk of change—for 27 years.

But nothing really important—for me and my kids—ever changes: the lesson plan books that no one ever really looks at and why should they? My lessons change by the second depending upon my interactions with my kids. This is not to imply that I don't have an overall objective in my head, or that I don't already know how I'm going to get there, but that is on me, moment by moment, and I've often thought that what we do is like the work of a surgeon who knows what the outcome of the operations should be, but does not always know what will happen or what new things will be discovered during the surgery. You just stay with it, and maybe the opera-tion doesn't come to a neat closure at the end of the specified time, but that's OK. The kids *will* stay with you, if they trust you, if they believe that you know where you're all going. All these little, neat ideas of what a perfect lesson should be from all these wonderful teachers who are no longer in the classroom, for whatever reason. *No.* Teaching is not neat. More often, it's messy. Kids have to reexamine what they thought to be true, in light of something that you've presented. They have to make it fit. Sometimes you get the "Aha! Now I get it." Other times, there's more confusion. But that's OK, that's when they do their best thinking, to make things work, to make things fit.

That's what *I've* been doing. I've been trying to make things under-standable, to make this career that I love, make sense. And I've confronted some powerful ideas (for me), and this process hasn't fit into our deadlines, and as I type this, make it *real*, I know that I could *only* have started it today, the day after summer school finished.

Yesterday, while I was waiting for my husband to pick me up at school, Jeramie (one of my students who had to go to summer school) sat outside and waited with me. He let me know three times that another one of his buses had gone by. I told him that he'd better get going to work, but each time he assured me that "No, it's OK."

Jeramie passed my class in summer school. He had also passed his English class in summer school, but he had also failed it, because he had not reached a certain benchmark in reading. This is one of the new interesting concepts that kids and parents will have to come to understand: yes, you passed, but you still failed. As if we knew that we could teach you, a ninth grader, how to read and all of the vocabulary that you've never learned (forget that English isn't even your first language) in 5 weeks of summer school, Monday through Thursday, 2 hours a day . . . and yet we do it.

Now, because Jeramie didn't reach the benchmark, he will be a ninth grader again. Forget that he passed all his other subjects. The new promotion policy says that if you don't pass a major subject, you get to keep the word *ninth grader* attached to your name.

Jeramie tells me, with a smile (again, the tears well up), that this is the third time he'll be kept back, "but that's OK." The only thing that he says won't be OK about it is that it means he'll be in the same class as his sister (an entering ninth grader). I tell him that they won't be in the same class (and I immediately think, "Big deal. A kid just tells you that he's 3 years behind in school, and you tell him that he won't be in the same class as his sister, to make him feel a little better at that moment.")

He told me, "But I'm *going to be* in your class again for math."

I told him that I wouldn't have him for math, because he had passed the course. He told me, "You watch. I'm going to be in your class." And I felt good (and the tears are streaming now because the older I get, the less it is about me feeling good about what I do, because I already feel good about my teaching). I don't need others telling me what I know. And I'm not sure if this is coming out right: I don't mean it to sound as though I'm this perfect teacher who can't learn from supervision, etc., but at this stage of the game, *I know whom I can learn from*, and I need to have some say in that. Do I feel some joy in Jeramie's telling me that he's going to be in my class? You don't know what that means to me, it means *everything* to me, because he's telling me that he learned, that he was important, *he is important*. And Sonia, this is *the secret*, the secret that Sonie is looking for.

When I called Sonie, she told me she was not going back to the inquiry group. She explained that she keeps going to the meetings, half expecting that at some point the (older) teachers in the group were going to open up and finally reveal their *secret*. . . . Like Sonie, I too was looking for the secret, I guess. I don't really remember what I said to Sonie on the phone when she brought up this idea of the *secret*. It was such a pure statement on her part, and at first I kind of thought, "If only it were so simple." And I knew that she knew that it wasn't. . . .

When I got off the phone with Sonie, I remembered some quote that I had hanging on the bulletin board in the kitchen (one of the thousands of pieces that I've ripped out of newspapers, magazines, all little pieces of my own search for "the secret"): "The secret of Life is to have a task, something you devote your entire life to, something you bring everything to . . . and the most important thing is—it must be something you cannot possibly do!" (Henry Moore).

God knows who Henry Moore is—was—but at the time, I felt, this is it, I'll give it to Sonie. It's about as good an answer to her quest (my quest?) for a secret as I can find. Now that I think about it, isn't this just what a young teacher would want to hear when thinking about how hard teaching is? Give your whole life to something that you can't possibly do!

I brought my little quote to our inquiry group retreat. *It was a perfect day. It was a perfect day.* I had to write it again, because it was. The weather was beautiful. The place was beautiful. We took pictures together.

I got there early. I had brought something about my burning question (for me, my burning question was still the question that got me into this group to begin with, Sonia's question: "What keeps [you] teachers going?"). On the way out of the house, I had grabbed a couple of little note cards (from a box of note cards I had picked up during April vacation, in order to write some thank you's to kids in school), thinking we could all sign them for Ceronne and Sonia. I was going to be prepared for this last meeting. I even sat and wrote while waiting for everyone to arrive. Of course, I wrote about how guilty I felt being surrounded by the flowers, etc., etc., etc., while my kids were stuck back at school in a building with windows that don't open, etc., etc., on this perfect May day.

Ceronne was next to arrive. We spoke for a few moments about "the place"; of course. I told her about my guilt, and then she gave me the permission to enjoy this day, without thinking about the kids in school. This was one of the gifts of the day: Someone in the system (i.e., part of the administration) said to a teacher, "Don't think about the kids, for today. Think about yourself." Of course, by thinking about ourselves, our practice, we *are* thinking about the kids. The line is so fine.

There were so many things about that day: the simple but profound truths in Freire's book; so many of the secrets, the ones that we know in our hearts, not really secrets after all; all the fears that each of us shared; all from teachers who, in front of their classes, I know, are confident teachers (would their students even/ever suspect how fearful we could be at times?)

We change lives forever. Driving home, thinking about the whole day, the verse on the front of the note card *hit* me. I bought them. I brought them to the meeting. I had looked at the verse: *We change lives forever.*

What power!

Of course, we all know it. But how often do we *really* think about it. Probably, subconsciously, more often than we admit. Does it get lost in the piles of paper that we correct? In the scores/grades that we write down? *Lives.* Jeramie's life, Sonie's life.

This has been another one of the group's gifts to me (lots of tears now . . .).

I knew when we were at the retreat that when I wrote, it would have to be about Sonie. I didn't know exactly what, but I asked her permission then.

When Sonie was my student in the ninth grade, I sent her to time-out more than any other student in my 27 years of teaching in the Boston public schools. Was she fresh? Not exactly. Disruptive? Not in the sense of how teachers usually think about disruptive students. Then why would I send her out? When I think back upon it, and I've talked to her about this, the only thing that I remember is that she would be acting "crazy" and I really don't remember how/what she did; I only remember that I could not allow her to stay in that room and act however it was that she was acting and allow other kids in her class to see and believe that this is who she was, because she was too bright. (In recent years, I've often thought about what would have happened now, since we no longer have time-out. She would have been returned to class, after a little "talking to" if lucky). I remember that she used to stay after school, as part of a homework-type club that another teacher and I held. Sometimes, we'd drive the kids to a bus station afterwards. Sometimes Sonie was one of the kids. We'd talk about different things after school. I remember Sonie telling us about a bedroom set that she was getting as a gift (didn't it have a canopy bed?). I can remember her "Hello, Miss." There was a spark to her. She was not one of those students to come in before school, to search you out to talk. Not one of those students who gave out the signals that they wanted you to dig deeper. At basketball games, she would chase my son around the gym, make him laugh; tease him, make him cry. She would always ask, "How's little Peter?" She still does, and she still gives me that little twinkle in her eye when she asks, as if we've gone back 13, 14, years.

When Sonie left the ninth-grade cluster, she was not one of those students who came back all the time to talk, to let you know what was going on in her life, what her plans were. We'd see each other in the hall, and we always asked after each other. "How's little Peter?" One year (junior? senior?), she gave me a book that she had written/made for an English project: *Why Cats Hate Water*, bound and covered with a piece of flowered, red flannel. Looking at it now, it looks so simple. I've treasured it. Now, I'm thinking about what Sonie, the teacher, would think about it: Would it receive a passing grade, according to the rubrics? Would she pass, but fail? Did this project show what she would become?

I remember Sonie as a senior, when she and a group of friends put on an assembly program, reading from/acting out works from Black women writers. And I remember having tears in my eyes because they were so good.

After that, I would see Sonie at games, but not that many. She would drop into school sometimes, when she was in college, but not that often. We didn't write, we didn't call. I had been her ninth-grade math teacher. She had been my student.

And then she was a teacher. *Sonie* became a teacher! (But she always must have been; I just hadn't noticed). Not only did Sonie become a teacher, but her first teaching assignment was with us, her ninth-grade teachers. And she was wonderful! And we had talks about her as a student and how we touched her life in ways that we never knew. We've cried over the passing of friends, who had also been our students; we've talked about parents who did the best that they could, both hers and mine: And I knew that we had made a difference in her life, just as my teachers had made a difference in my life.

In the teaching autobiography I wrote, I talked about being the oldest of eight, and knowing that the nuns that I had in school made the difference in my life. And I know that I received their special attention because I was bright; I always did what Sister said, unlike Sonie! I've always respected those kids who do not say, "Yes, Miss" in words or actions all of the time; there's a spark in them that I never wanted to extinguish. I know that there were others in my family who didn't get the same type of attention from Sister (who at the time, to be fair, had about 38 students in a class). What difference did it make in their lives? Did someone extinguish their spark? or worse, ignore it?

I always knew teachers made a difference, a tremendous difference, and I've always taken the responsibility very seriously, but to think about it using these words: *Teachers change lives forever* and ever . . . and ever . . . lives . . . To really think about *that*, for a long time, is frightening, that type of power, to use it day after day . . . .

In our inquiry group, by talking about our practice, we allowed the possibility of different words to enter into/shape the conversations among us, between us, and within our own minds, about what we do every day. This was the power of the group.

The possibility of using different words to talk about the day-in-day-out experiences of 20-plus years—Junia's "revolution"; Steve's night-before-going-back-to-school jitters; Judith's questioning of herself vis-à-vis the young men in her classes; Claudia's new dialogues with her students; Ambrizeth's teaching which involves a culture within a culture . . . .

When I got home from the inquiry group meeting after Sonie read her autobiography, I collapsed in a chair and cried, and cried, and cried. I told my husband that that was it. I could stop teaching now and knew that I had done what I was supposed to do (such drama, Karen!). I had heard Sonie's story, and it was also my story. I thought about the teachers I had had, who saw something in the "disadvantaged kids" from the city, and gave us the hope that we could do whatever we wanted, and more important, we could do it without giving up who we were. We didn't have to move to the suburbs to be successful. (I laugh when I recall the neighborhood priest who one day referred to our high school as "St. Augustine's Academy for Girls, by the Sea"—if you ever saw our school, this name was the furthest thing from truth! I only remember him saying it a couple of times but, to this day, when any of the girls from my class get together, we all remember it: a time when someone made us feel "special"). We could still be of the city, of the streets. But I also thought about all of us who weren't singled out for any special attention, who got lost, literally, in the crowd. And I think of Jeramie, kept back for the third time in his life. And he smiles and says, "But that's OK." It's *not* OK. We need different words to speak about what we do. Standards. Rubrics. Benchmarks. Ninth grader. Important words, yes. *But* . . . These words do not tell the complete stories of our kids; they do not tell the complete stories of what we do. *We change lives forever.*

We are going to change lives forever, one way or another, for good or for bad. When we talked in the group about our anger, this is where it's coming from. When we talked about our frustrations, this is where it's coming from. When we talk about leaving the profession, this is where it's coming from: We change lives forever. Are we doing all that can be done? Smaller class sizes, access to the latest (forget latest—*any*) technology. Our school was wired for computers 10 years ago. We never got computers, but this summer, it's being rewired for *faster* Internet access. Yet still no computers in my classroom, no computer lab to meet the individual strengths/weaknesses of my kids who must go to summer school, because *they* can't meet the standards.

So, despite everything in our way, why do some of us end up staying? Is it because *our* lives continue to be changed forever, for the better, by our students? What would my life be without Sonie, without Jeramie? It's not a give-and-take; it's a cycle, just as learning isn't the first step, then the second. In most cases, it's learning, retracing, reworking. Is the light in their eyes a reflection of the light in *our* eyes, or is it just the opposite? It is an addictive thing, teaching. Once your life has been changed, you understand the power.

I saw Sonie before the end of the year, and I told her that I had looked up one of the teachers who had made a difference in my life, who had changed *my* life forever. She was now living in Birmingham, Alabama, and she was still teaching. And I told her about the past year in the inquiry group, and about Sonie, about being in this group with a teacher who had also been a student of mine. I told her what her being my teacher had meant for me. As we spoke, she would recall bits of conversations that we had had when I was in the seventh grade. They weren't about science, which was what she taught, or about me as a student in her science class. She remembered things that I had told her about my baby sister, offbeat, personal things (like I remember about Sonie's bedroom set). I thanked her (just as I thank Sonie for helping me to look for the secret).

Sonia, I'm not going to read this over now. I'm going to send it right out. Please forgive typos, etc., etc. I know that I just went on and on. But now it's out, and my head feels empty. Hopefully, I'll be able to be "on vacation" before school starts up again, without all these thoughts popping up whenever. At some point, I may even reread what I wrote and think, Oh, my God, what did I say? I know that it is way past June 12, but I wanted you to know what the work in the group has meant to me. Keep changing our (teachers' and students') lives forever. Thank you.

P.S. I'll always remember sitting in the room with the snacks on retreat day. You were talking about being on a panel with "names" that you looked up to at a certain conference. I could see the light in your eyes, and I asked you if at those times you think about that little Puerto Rican girl from New York. Our kids need to hear that we are still them.

TEACHERS CHANGE LIVES FOREVER

It's interesting to me that Karen ended her letter in this way. It helped me think about the teachers who changed my life forever. There was the fourth-grade teacher who, when I said I wanted to go to college (who knows where I got that idea from? Nobody in my family had even graduated from high school), encouraged me, even in a neighborhood where few children knew what college was. But in the same breath, she remarked that we still needed "people to clean toilets," such a devastatingly cruel statement. I'm sure she didn't intend it to be cruel; she just wanted us to know that it was

OK if not everybody went to college. But what did the children hear when she said that?

There was my ninth-grade science teacher, Mr. Slotkin, who made science (of all things! a subject in which I had never excelled) both fascinating and exciting. There were Mr. and Mrs. Fried, both French teachers in my high school, who gave me great affirmation and support and nurtured my lifelong love for languages. For the first time in my life, in their classrooms, I knew that speaking Spanish was no disgrace; in fact, it was even an asset. (Perhaps it is no surprise that my older daughter is now a teacher of French and Spanish). And there were also teachers who said, "You're different from the other Puerto Ricans," as if they were doing me a favor, and there were others who seemed genuinely surprised that I was intelligent. Teachers do indeed change lives every day.

Chapter 9

FINAL THOUGHTS: WHAT KEEPS TEACHERS GOING IN SPITE OF EVERYTHING?

Building learning community into the work lives of American high school teaching is fundamentally a problem of reculturing the profession— changing the ethos of teaching from individualism to collaboration, from conservatism to innovation.

Milbrey McLaughlin and Joan Talbert, *Professional Communities and the Work of High School Teachers*

A major finding in the multiyear study of American high schools by Milbrey McLaughlin and Joan Talbert referred to above is that most high schools lack strong communities of practice (an absence certainly not confined to high schools).[1] The teachers in the What Keeps Teachers Going inquiry group, as well as many other teachers with whom I've worked over the years, would probably agree that having such a community would be a positive incentive to keep going. This is not a new concern: as early as 1975, Dan Lortie suggested that developing a professional community would benefit not just individual teachers but the profession as a whole.[2] The question is how to promote such communities in a context of restructuring and standardization that gives little thought to teacher learning and support. That is the subject of this final reflection.

After participating in the inquiry group, I decided to ask other teachers with whom I've worked to react to the question of what keeps them going. What most of them have told me, and what a small number subsequently wrote, confirmed that they agreed with much of what we found through the inquiry group project. Since the ending of the project, I've shared our insights with many other teachers around the country. Most have agreed with what we found, and they have done so enthusiastically. As a result, I have come to believe that the conclusions we reached reflect the experiences of many teachers, not just of one small group of teachers from Boston, Massachusetts, who met monthly for a year to discuss big and important questions about teacher resilience, student learning, and, in effect, the future of public education in the United States.

I've also learned that talking about what keeps teachers in the profession is emotional stuff. When I've met with other teachers and I've told them about the inquiry group or shared what the teachers had written, many have been inspired to tell their own stories about teaching and some have been moved to tears. At the same time, I do not claim that all teachers in all schools everywhere will agree with everything that the teachers in this book assert. Teachers are too diverse, their circumstances too various, to make any such claim. I do think, however, that we've uncovered some kernels of truth from which all teachers, and the profession as a whole, can benefit.

LESSONS FROM THE WORK OF TEACHERS

Even before I started this project, I was fairly certain that I knew from my own experience some of the reasons that teachers enter and remain in the profession: the students, of course; a desire to be part of a meaningful and worthwhile endeavor; the possibility that their work might have an impact on the future. These things turned out to be true, but working with the teachers in the inquiry group also gave me a language with which to articulate some ideas about teaching that had until then been lying just under the surface of my consciousness. Some of them surprised me, for example, that joy and hope can be the other side of anger and desperation and that all these emotions may be experienced by committed teachers at different points in their careers and even at different times of the day. Some things didn't surprise me as much as enlighten me, for example, the tremendous effort involved in doing the intellectual work of teaching. Other ideas reinforced my own practice as a teacher educator, especially the notion that teaching is first and foremost about relationships with students and colleagues.

The teachers included in the book are an unusually committed and talented group. Not all teachers are like them, nor should all teachers need to mirror the same single-minded dedication and enormous energy of this group. All teachers, however, can learn from the lessons we learned, lessons that I briefly review below.

Developing the stance that teaching is an intellectual endeavor, one that needs constant nurturing and attention, is one such lesson. This point was made explicit in the reflections of Patty Bode and Stephen Gordon, but it was evident as well in the words of many others. Deciding how and what to teach is hard work, at times even agonizing. Keeping abreast of the newest developments in one's specific subject takes time. It can also be exhausting, as we saw when Mary Cowhey described the physics course she took. But in the end, becoming and staying smart are part of the very fabric of the profession. If all teachers thought of their work in this way, there would be no limit to what we could expect from them and consequently from their students.

Another lesson that can benefit all teachers is that *teaching is about— and for—democracy*. For the teachers in this book, teaching is a way of making concrete the ideals that are the very bedrock of our civilization. When Junia Yearwood teaches students about their rights and responsibilities as citizens of a democratic society, her curriculum goes beyond simply reiterating a noble principle in history books. Her students' letter to the editor, for example, was not just an academic exercise. Although the activity no doubt reinforced students' skills in writing a persuasive letter free of grammatical and spelling errors, it accomplished something much more significant. It taught the students the power of the written word and underlined the need to *practice* democracy, not just talk about it. Many of the stories in this book reinforce the fact that dedicated and excellent teachers find many ways to focus on equality and democracy as part of their pedagogy and curriculum.

In a related vein, understanding that *teaching necessarily involves love and respect* is a major theme that emerged in the work of these committed teachers. Rather than shy away from this element of teaching, they accept it as a given. But instead of thinking that loving students means being easygoing and indulgent, successful teachers believe just the opposite: that it is with even more urgency that they place high demands on students, especially those who others may not believe are capable.

Autobiography is part of teaching, and this too was clear in our work in the inquiry group. Whether it is their own identities or the experiences they had as young people or even later in their lives, these can make a difference in teachers' staying power. Autobiography, however, is not destiny. That is, being a member of any specific group, or being brought up with particular values, neither limits nor guarantees one's possibilities in life. Certainly the fact that Junia grew up thinking about the injustices created by chattel slavery influenced her decision to become a teacher, and it has strengthened her resolve to remain in teaching and serve the young people of Boston. The fact that Steve Gordon grew up in a household with certain values about equality and fair play no doubt influenced him to become a teacher. But one does not have to grow up in such circumstances to become a dedicated teacher. For some teachers, cultural identity had little to do with becoming a teacher. Some people found themselves in situations that led them to teaching by accident. For example, Claudia Bell, although not

Hispanic herself, became a bilingual teacher because of a positive experience working with adult Hispanic immigrants hungry for education.

The work of teachers in the inquiry group also supports the notion that talk itself is a form of learning that can lead to change in thoughts and actions. This means that *creating communities of learning among teachers is necessary if they are to remain connected to their profession, their students, and one another.* The truth of this statement was evident throughout the year in which the inquiry group met, but it was especially obvious during our final meeting. Several of the teachers in the group spoke of the difference it had made to them that they had colleagues to call on throughout the year. Although teaching remains a lonely profession, the teachers no longer felt as if they were walking into their classrooms alone. When they experience a close companionship among their peers, teachers often feel as if their colleagues—or at least their colleagues' wisdom and insights—are walking in with them. The power of creating such communities of inquiry is one of the most important lessons we learned that year.

These lessons have consequences for all teachers because all of them can learn from excellent teachers who remain in the profession. In fact, all of us, whether teachers, teacher educators, parents, or the general public, can gain from what the teachers in this book know and do. In what follows, I consider just two implications from our thinking and dialogue.

RETHINKING PROFESSIONAL DEVELOPMENT

Rethinking professional development means changing how teachers are prepared for the profession in the first place, and changing the conditions in which they continue to learn throughout their careers. In other words, it means a major shift in the culture of teacher preparation. While schools and colleges of education have changed their practices in the past several decades to incorporate newer research and pedagogy as well as more relevant field placements, it is still too often the case that many new teachers enter the profession with very little idea of what to expect in teaching.[3] Teacher education cannot do it all, of course, and no amount of courses or field placements can prepare new teachers with what it is really like to walk into a classroom and teach. But they can do more.

For one, teacher preparation needs to shift its focus from questions of *what* and *how* to also consider questions of *why*. That is, the emphasis of some teacher education programs on strategies and techniques does little to prepare teachers to understand that these are just a small part of teaching. True, it is necessary to know a variety of approaches and to experiment with them and feel confident in one's ability to use them. But teaching is far more than specific procedures; it is a way of thinking about learning, and of one's students, and of what will be most useful for them. Steve Gordon brought this point out vividly during one of our inquiry group meetings. Exasperated with the current focus on "best practices," as if such practices are "best" in every case and for all students, he asked, "What about *loving* practices?" This question made a lot of sense to us.

All teachers, whether new or veteran, also need to know more about the students they teach. Our public urban schools are increasingly filled by students whose lives and experiences are vastly different from those of their teachers, who are overwhelmingly White, middle class, and mono-lingual English-speakers. Most know very little, either from direct experience or training, about the diversity of their students. If this is the case, they may become frustrated and impatient, longing for an idealized past that never was, when all children were easy to teach and looked like them. Unless we prepare new teachers with the kinds of experiences that equip them to go into diverse urban schools with both level-headedness and hope, the situation will remain the same.

Excellent teachers don't develop full-blown at graduation; nor are they just "born teachers." Instead, teachers are always in the process of "becoming." Given the dynamics of their work, they need to continually rediscover who they are and what they stand for through their dialogue and collaboration with peers, through ongoing and consistent study, and through deep reflection about their craft. They also need to understand the nature of their work and its life-and-death potential in the lives of their students. They need to understand that teaching is neither missionary work (although it may be a mission), nor just another job.

Moreover, schools and colleges of education, as well as school districts and state departments of education (all of which are increasingly involved in teacher education), need to recruit a more diverse teaching population in the first place. The cultural congruency between teachers and students is no guarantee that students will learn better or more effectively, but having a teaching force that is more representative of our general population can certainly help. And, as recent research has pointed out, it is not just students of color who benefit from the presence of a more diverse teaching faculty, but all students.[4]

Another essential—although increasingly scarce—condition necessary for teacher learning is *time*. In my work with teachers, this is the one issue on which almost all agree—there simply is not enough time in the day to do all that they need to do. Aside from the typical obligations to plan curriculum and grade papers, more and more teachers are understanding the need to collaborate with peers, engage in intellectual inquiry, and keep abreast of the latest research and trends. But most schools do little to help these things happen. In most, professional development is defined as bringing in experts to do a workshop. Sometimes school districts send teachers to attend a conference, but this is not very common. Paying for them to do so is even more unlikely. Also rare are opportunities for teachers to plan together or to participate in reading or inquiry groups. If the culture of teacher preparation is to change, one way to begin is to advance the model of teacher-as-intellectual. This means providing *time and support* for teachers to meet and work together.

RESTRUCTURING SCHOOLS

The second implication of our work is directly related to the first: If schools are to become places where teachers find community and engage in intellectual work, they need to provide environments that help teachers do these things. This idea is neither new nor earth shattering; research has found that changing the structures of schools to promote teacher development also promotes student learning.[5] This is not to say that intellectual work is easy, or even always welcome by teachers. It is, as many of the teachers in the inquiry group said, sometimes painful and difficult, but it is also a necessary and crucial part of teaching. If teachers cannot practice intellectual work in schools, they simply fall back on clichés or on tried-and-true practices that may be ill-suited for their students. Karen Gelzinis explained it this way: "It is much easier to live this teaching life without the reflection. And it is so easy to avoid the reflection, because there is always something to do; the bag is never empty. Even at the end of the term, as you're wrapping up grades, the work from the new term is already piling up, and you are behind again."

Just as schools need to restructure to promote intellectual engagement among teachers, they also need to do so as a hedge against the massive teacher shortage that is fast approaching. A recent study, for instance, found that teacher recruitment programs will do little to solve the coming teacher shortage unless they also address the organizational structure of schools, because they are part of the reason that teachers leave in the first place. These structures are not about "reform" writ large, that is, reform in such areas as standardized testing and vouchers. Instead, they include such simple strategies as providing teachers with opportunities to have input into school decision-making and raising teacher salaries.[6] Yet as a nation, we continue to rely on large, comprehensive reforms grafted onto schools with little thought as to how they might work in that context. Such large-scale reforms have shown mixed results at best.[7]

It is no easy task to create the kind of environment in which authentic learning communities can take hold. Most schools are not structured to sustain fellowship. More often than not, consciously or by coincidence, many schools are organized to encourage only competition and individual excellence. They are sometimes like individual fiefdoms: classrooms in which teachers rule, headed by an overall lord who calls the shots in the school, a "downtown" that determines what takes place in the district, and a local or state board that makes policy for all of them. It is the kind of structure that works against community, making it too easy to retreat into personal spaces.

Moreover, teaching as intellectual engagement requires constant nurturing and guidance. It is not an activity learned once and put aside. Teaching as intellectual work means looking collaboratively and critically at student work and talking together about what works and what doesn't work; it means developing curriculum with other teachers and having the opportunity to discuss thought-provoking books and ideas. Teaching seen in this way is arduous intellectual work, the kind of work that makes teaching an exciting exertion, a "beautiful life," as Steve Gordon described it at one of our meetings.

Supporting professional development also must challenge teachers' perceptions and biases without moralizing or blaming. An isolated workshop simply won't do, nor will attending one conference or taking one university course a year. Teachers need to give sustained attention to the problems and possibilities of their classrooms and schools. This means teachers need to be provided with money, time, books, and other resources. Equally essential, teachers need to be involved in setting the agenda for their own learning. Simply providing workshops, seminars, or other professional development in which teachers have no say, no matter how timely or well intentioned, is doomed to fail.

The thrill of intellectually stimulating work for the teachers in the inquiry group was evident at every meeting. In spite of the late hour, the bureaucratic frustrations, and the looming lesson plans to be written and papers to be graded later that evening, most participants were exhilarated by our discussions. Many spoke about the pressing need for more such conversations and they wanted to share their insights and struggles with new teachers. New teachers have much to learn from them. But learning from a handful of teachers—exceedingly talented as they may be—is not enough to change the educational landscape for millions of our students in public schools. It will take sustained effort, a strong will, and tremendous resources to improve our public schools so that all young people can benefit. One way to begin this difficult task is by creating the conditions under which they are free to do their best.

DEVELOPING NEW NATIONAL PRIORITIES FOR TEACHING

It is by now a truism that the profession of teaching, although enormously significant in the lives of so many people, is terribly undervalued, undercompensated, and underrespected. We see signs of this everywhere: Teachers take second jobs as cashiers in convenience stores and clean houses during their summer vacations; they spend hundreds and sometimes thousands of dollars of their own money each year on classroom materials; and they spend even more on their continuing education, usually with no compensation from their school districts. Yet the current policy climate at both state and national levels is permeated by a profound disrespect for teachers, especially teachers in urban schools, and for the children they teach. Most politicians, for instance, although they speak often about education, rarely step foot in schools. They tend to stress only accountability, and the tone they use to speak about teachers is sometimes disparaging and unforgiving. But no first-year signing bonus, no teacher test, and no high-stakes test can take the place of a true, enduring respect for teachers. In fact, these things often get in the way of retaining good teachers because they question the intelligence, ability, and commitment of teachers.

One thing we learned from the inquiry group project that we are certain about is this: *No amount of decontextualized "best practices" will keep teachers engaged or committed.* The current discourse in educational reform focuses on developing "best practices" as the antidote to both teacher burnout and student underachievement. Our work departs in an essential way from this stance. We have come to the conclusion that it is only when teachers are treated as professionals and intellectuals who care deeply about their students and their craft that they will be enticed to remain in the profession and that new teachers will be attracted to join. We hope that our work illustrates that, rather than a focus on dehumanized "best practices," we need to focus on students and those who best teach them.

Teachers who keep going in spite of everything know that teaching is more than a job. Junia Yearwood's thoughts about teaching probably reflect this idea best:

> Maintaining my enjoyment and passion for teaching for over
> 20 years can be attributed to several reasons, two of which include
> the love and respect I have for my students and my personal need
> to remain intellectually alive. However, the principal reason why I
> continue to enter the classroom with energy and a sense of hope lies
> in how I view what I do. Teaching is not just my profession; it is my
> calling; it is my mission.

Teachers such as Junia need to be supported by teacher educators, administrators, school committees, politicians, and citizens who care about and support with words, deeds, and money the work of schools in our society. If we are really serious about expanding the opportunities for students in our urban public schools, rather than concentrating on high-stakes tests, we should be focusing our efforts on high standards, high expectations, and high finance.

This is the challenge that lies ahead. If we are as concerned about education as we say we are, then we need to do more to change the conditions faced by teachers, especially those who work in underfinanced and largely abandoned urban schools. We need to support those teachers who love their students, who find creative ways to teach them, and who do so under difficult circumstances. We need to celebrate teachers who are as excited about their own learning as they are about the learning of their students. And we need to champion those teachers who value their students' families and find respectful ways to work with them. Above all, we need to expect all teachers to do these things. The children in our public schools deserve no less.

NOTES

Introduction

1. P. H. B. Shin, (2001, June 19), "Teachers Are Key to Success: It's Sink or Swim for Class Rookies," *New York Daily News* (http://www.nydailynews.com/City_Beat/a-115421.asp).

2. The Public Education Network and *Education Week* (2001, April), *Action for All: The Public's Responsibility for Public Education* (Washington, DC: Authors).

3. M. W. McLaughlin & J. E. Talbert (2001), *Professional Ccommunities and the Work of High School Teaching* (Chicago: University of Chicago Press).

4. Jane David and Patrick Shields report that many teachers are teaching "out of field," particularly in schools serving poor children (J. L. David & P. M. Shields [2001], *When Theory Hits Reality: Standards-Based Reform in Urban Districts, Final Narrative Report.* [Menlo Park, CA: SRI International]). In California, for example, the number of unqualified teachers increased from 34,000 in 1997 to 42,000 in 2001, accounting for 14% of the teaching force and effectively undermining that state's reform efforts such as reduced class size. (D. Helfand [2001, December 12], "Lack of Qualified Teachers Undermines State Reforms" *Los Angeles Times* [online], available: www.latimes.com/news/local/la-0000986.50dec12.story?coll=la%2Dcalifornia). For a national perspective, see L. Darling-Hammond (1998), "Teachers and Teaching: Testing Policy Hypotheses From a National Commission Report," *Educational Researcher, 27*(1), 5–15.

5. In its 1996 report, the National Commission on Teaching and America's Future, for instance, begins with the premise that "what teachers know and do is one of the most important influences on what students learn." See National Commission on Teaching and America's Future (1996), *What Matters Most: Teaching for America's Future.* (New York: Author). Additionally, Linda Darling-Hammond and Beverly Falk, in reviewing dozens of studies on retention in the late 1990s, have suggested that until schools address the enormous inequalities in students' access to qualified teachers, other changes will have little effect on student achievement (L. Darling-Hammond & B. Falk (1997), "Using Standards and Assessments to Support Student Learning," *Phi Delta Kappan, 79*(3), 190–199). Finally, a recent study by Judith Langer found that student achievement in reading, writing, and English among middle and high school students is related to skills their teachers possess. Most impressive was the finding that students in some schools demonstrated higher literacy achievement levels *than their demographically comparable counterparts.* Langer evaluated 88 classes in Florida, New York, California, and Texas over a period of 2 years. See J. Langer (2002), "Beating the Odds: Teaching

Middle and High School Students to Read and Write Well," *American Educational Research Journal*, *38*(4), 837–880.

6. K. Haycock (1998), "Good Teaching Matters," *Thinking K-16*, *3*(2), 1–2.

7. A. Hargreaves, L. Earl, & J. Ryan (1996), *Schooling for Change*. (New York: Falmer Press).

8. N. Noddings (1992), *The Challenge to Care in Schools: An Alternative Approach to Education* (New York: Teachers College Press), p. 2.

9. National Center for Education Statistics (2000), *Editorial Projects in Education, 1998*. (Washington, DC: Author).

10. See R. R. Henke, S. P. Choy, X. Chen, S. Geis, & M. N. Alt (1997), *America's Teachers: Profile of a Profession, 1993–94, NCES 97-460* (Washington, DC: United States Department of Education). For a comparison of race/ethnicity of teachers from 1961 through 1996, see T. D. Snyder & C. M. Hoffman (2002), *Digest of Education Statistics, 2001* (Washington, DC: National Center for Education Statistics). For projections of changes in the teaching force, see United States Bureau of the Census (2000), *Statistical Abstract of the United States* [online], available: http://www.census.gov/prod/www/statistical-abstract-us.html. In addition, in a recent study investigating the pipeline to teaching, researchers found that the major challenge of creating a racially and ethnically diverse teaching force is *not* primarily one of influencing the occupational decisions of college graduates of color, but rather of increasing the high school graudation, and later, college enrollment and graduation, of students of diverse backgrounds. See E. Vegas, R. J. Murname & J. B. Willett (2001), "From High School to Teaching: Many Steps, Who Makes It? *Teachers College Record*, *103*(3), 427–449.

11. See, for example, T. S. Dee (2000), *Teachers, Race, and Student Achievement in a Randomized Experiment* (Cambridge, MA: National Bureau of Economic Research); and B. C. Clewell, M. Puma & S. A. McKay (2001), *Does It Matter If My Teacher Looks Like Me? The Impact of Teacher Race and Ethnicity on Student Academic Achievement* (New York: Ford Foundation).

12. In a recent study that examined the 350 largest culturally diverse school districts in Texas, researchers found a positive relationship between the number of teachers of color and the achievement of students of color. What surprised them was that the relationship between the number of teachers of color and the achievement of Anglo students was *even higher* (K. J. Meier, R. D. Wrinkle, & J. L. Polinard (1999), "Representative Bureaucracy and Distributional Equity: Addressing the Hard Question," *Journal of Politics*, *61*, 1025–1039).

13. This and other early research is included in the report of a national symposium sponsored by Phi Delta Kappan and the National Education Association's National Commission on Teacher Education and Professional Standards (T. M. Stinnett (ed.) (1970), *The Teacher Dropout* (Bloomington, IN: Phi Delta Kappan). See also R. R. Henke, X. Chen, & S. Geis (2000), *Progress Through the Teacher Pipeline: 1992 – 1992 College Graduates and Elementary/Secondary School Teaching as of 1997* (Washington, DC: National Center for Education Statistics).

14. From 1987 to 1989, for example, nearly 12% of teachers with less than a year's experience left the classroom, while from 1993 to 1995, the rate had risen to 22%. Those who left teaching after 3 years represented almost 9% of the teaching

force from 1987 to 1989, but more than 12% from 1993 to 1995. More recently, about 20% of those who started teaching in 1993 had left the field by 1997. More revealing yet is the following: Over the span of 4 decades, from the 1960s to the 1990s, when teachers were asked whether they would be willing to teach again, the percentage answering in the affirmative decreased from more than 75% in 1961 to only 62% in 1996 (National Center for Education Statistics [2000], *Digest of Education Statistics, 1999* [Washington, DC: Author], p. 82).

15. M. Haberman (1995), "Selecting 'Star' Teachers for Children and Youth in Urban Poverty, *Phi Delta Kappan*, 76(10), 777–781. Further, recent research is confirming that teachers are leaving the profession for other jobs. See Education Commission of the States (2000), *In Pursuit of Quality Teaching: Five Key Strategies for Policymakers* (Denver, CO: Education Commission of the States). On the rate of teachers leaving schools in poor areas, see K. Haycock (1998), "No More Settling for Less, *Thinking K–16*, 4(1), 3–12.

16. Richard Ingersoll calls the phenomenon of teachers who move from school to school via voluntary or involuntary transfer "migration." See R. M. Ingersoll (2001), *A Different Approach to Solving the Teacher Shortage Problem*, policy Brief no. 3 (Seattle, WA: Center for the Study of Teaching and Policy, University of Washington).

17. Depending on the assumptions made, projections for the number of newly hired public school teachers needed by 2009 range from 1.7 million to 2.7 million. See W. J. Hussar (1999), *Predicting the Need for Newly Hired Teachers in the United States to 2008–2009* (Washington, DC: National Center for Education Statistics).

18. See D. Wadsworth (2001), "Why New Teachers Choose to Teach," *Educational Leadership*, 58(8), 24–28.

19. The average school salary for public school teachers grew slowly during the 1990s, reaching $40,582 in 1998–99. After adjusting for inflation, this represents an increase of 1% between 1988 and 1999. See http://nces.ed.gov/pubs2001/digest/ch2.html.

20. As reported in a study provided to *Time* magazine by the research firm Quality Education Data, a division of Scholastic. See http://www.time.com/time/magazine/notebook0,9484,11010,20224,00.html.

21. S. M. Johnson (1990), *Teachers at Work: Achieving Success in Our Schools* (New York: Basic Books), p. 34. Also, a recent study by Public Agenda of nearly 900 teachers in public and private schools found that an impressive 865 believed that only those with "a true calling" should be teachers, while 72% said that what was most important in teaching was contributing to society and helping others. See S. Farkas, J. Johnson & T. Foleno (2000), *A Sense of Calling: Who Teaches and Why* (New York: Public Agenda).

22. G. Orfield, & J. T. Yun (1999, June), *Resegregation in American Schools* (Cambridge, MA: Civil Rights Project at Harvard University).

23. M. Rose (1995), *Possible Lives: The Promise of Public Education in America* (New York: Penguin Books), p. 1.

24. Neither teachers' writing, nor research done collaboratively with teachers, is new, although its popularity is growing for obvious reasons: The knowl-

edge and wisdom of experienced teachers can improve conditions in schools for everyone—children, other teachers, teacher educators, and other professional educators. Among the books in the genre that I have found most helpful are K. Casey (1993), *I Answer With My Life: Life Histories of Women Teachers Working for Social Change* (New York: Routledge); D. J. Clanindin, A. Davies, P. Hogan & B. Kennard (1993), *Learning to Teach, Teaching to Learn: Stories of Collaboration in Teacher Education* (New York: Teachers College Press); M. Cochran-Smith & S. Lytle (1993), *Inside/Outside: Teacher Research and Knowledge* (New York: Teachers College Press); R. F. Fox (ed.) (2000), *Case Studies in Teacher Renewal* (Urbana, IL: National Council of Teachers of English); S. W. Freedman, E. R. Simons, J. S. Kalnin, A. Casareno & the M-CLASS Teams (eds.) (1999), *Inside City Schools: Investigating Literacy in Multicultural Classrooms* (New York: Teachers College Press); M. Rose (1995), *Possible Lives: The Promise of Public Education in America* (Boston: Houghton Mifflin); C. Witherell & N. Noddings (eds.) (1991), *Stories Lives Tell: Narrative and Dialogue in Education* (New York: Teachers College Press); and S. M. Intrator (ed.) (2002), *Stories of the Courage to Teach: Honoring the Teacher's Heart* (San Francisco: Jossey-Bass).

Chapter 1

1. P. Freire (1970), *Pedagogy of the Oppressed* (New York: Seabury Press).

2. I. Shor & P. Freire, (1987), *A Pedagogy for Liberation: Dialogues on Transforming Education* (New York: Bergin & Garvey), p. 46.

3. These are the words of Sandra Stotsky, a vehement opponent of multicultural education, in her (1999) book *Losing Our Language: How Multicultural Classroom Instruction Is Undermining Our Children's Ability to Read, Write, and Reason* (New York: The Free Press). For proponents' explanation of the vehemence of the attack on multicultural education, see my (1995) chapter "From Brown Heroes and Holidays to Assimilationist Agendas: Reconsidering the Critiques of Multicultural Education," in C. E. Sleeter & P. McLaren (eds.), *Multicultural Education, Critical Pedagogy, and the Politics of Difference* (pp. 191–220) (Albany: State University of New York Press); and Christine Sleeter's (2001) chapter, "An Analysis of the Critiques of Multicultural Education," in J. A. Banks & C. A. M. Banks (eds.), *Handbook of Research on Multicultural Education* (pp. 81–94) (San Francisco: Jossey-Bass).

4. S. Bowles & H. Gintis (1976), *Schooling in Capitalist America: Educational Reform and the Contradictions of Economic Life.* (New York: Basic Books).

5. P. Freire (1970), *Pedagogy of the Oppressed* (New York: Seabury Press); M. Greene (1978), *Landscapes of Learning* (New York: Teachers College Press); H. Kohl (1967), *36 Children* (New York: New American Library); J. Kozol (1967). *Death at an Early Age: The Destruction of the Hearts and Minds of Negro Children in the Boston Public Schools* (Boston: Houghton Mifflin); S. Ashton-Warner (1963), *Teacher* (New York: Simon and Schuster). For early work in multicultural education, see J. A. Banks (ed.) (1973), *Teaching Ethnic Studies: Concepts and Strategies*, 43rd yearbook (Washington, DC: National Council for the Social Studies).

6. See, for example, J. Spring (2001), *Deculturalization and the Struggle for Equality: A Brief History of the Education of Dominated Cultures in the United States*, 3rd ed.(New York: McGraw-Hill).

7. S. Nieto (2000), *Affirming Diversity: The Sociopolitical Context of Multicultural Education*, 3rd ed. (New York: Longman [1st ed., 1992]).

8. P. Freire (1998), *Teachers as Cultural Workers: Letters to Those Who Dare Teach* (Boulder, CO: Westview Press), pp. 6, 36.

9. S. Nieto (1999), *The Light in Their Eyes: Creating Multicultural Learning Communities* (New York: Teachers College Press).

10. B. Campuzano (2001), "A Better Chance" *Narratives*, 6(1), 25–26.

Chapter 2

1. S. Buckley (2000, February 2), "Root of All Evil: Money Makes the Sports World Go Round," *Boston Herald*, p. 102.

2. b. hooks (1994), *Teaching to Transgress: Education as the Practice of Freedom* (New York: Routledge), p. 107.

3. L. Gibson (1998), "Teaching as an Encounter With the Self: Unraveling the Mix of Personal Beliefs, Education Ideologies, and Pedagogical Practices," *Anthropology and Education Quarterly*, 29(3), 360–371.

4. Some helpful books in this area are J. S. Bruner (1983), *In Search of Mind: Essays in Autobiography* (New York: Harper & Row); R. M. Cohen & S. Scheer (eds.) (1997), *The Work of Teachers in America: A Social History Through Stories* (New York: Longman); F. M. Connelly & D. J. Clandinin (1999), *Shaping a Professional Identity: Stories of Educational Practice* (New York: Teachers College Press); P. Dominicé (2000), *Learning From Our Lives: Using Educational Biographies With Adults* (San Francisco: Jossey-Bass). In addition, the journal *Narratives*, published by the Learning Communities Network, Inc., in Cleveland, Ohio, is a good source of stories concerning teaching that are written by both educators and students.

5. J. Bruner (1994), "Life as Narrative," in A. H. Dyson & C. Genishi (eds.), *The Need for Story: Cultural Diversity in Classroom and Community* (pp. 28–37) (Urbana, IL: National Council of Teachers of English).

6. M. Dickeman (1973), "Teaching Cultural Pluralism," in J. A. Banks (ed.), *Teaching Ethnic Studies: Concepts and Strategies* (pp. 4–25), 43rd yearbook (Washington, DC: National Council for the Social Studies).

7. Marilyn Cochran-Smith has also written about how she asks preservice teachers to "rewrite their autobiographies." See M. Cochran-Smith (2000), "Blind Vision: Unlearning Racism in Teacher Education." *Harvard Educational Review*, 70(2), 157–190.

8. J. Kozol (1991), *Savage Inequalities: Children in America's Schools* (New York: Crown).

9. S. Nieto (1999), *The Light in Their Eyes: Creating Multicultural Learning Communities* (New York: Teachers College Press).

10. G. W. Noblitt (1993), "Power and Caring," *American Educational Research Journal*, 3(1), 23–38.

11. L. D. Delpit (1988), "The Silenced Dialogue: Power and Pedagogy in Educating Other People's Children, *Harvard Educational Review*, 58, 280–298.

12. J. L. Miller (1978, May), *An Interview with Maxine Greene*, videotape (The Curriculum Collection, Museum of Education, University of South Carolina).

Chapter 3

1. The following are works by some of the many researchers who have investigated the characteristics of effective teachers of culturally and linguistically diverse students: E. E. García (1999), *Student Cultural Diversity: Understanding and Meeting the Challenge* (Boston: Houghton Mifflin); M. Haberman (1988), *Preparing Teachers for Urban Schools* (Bloomington, IN: Phi Delta Kappa Educational Foundation); G. Gordon (1999), "Teacher Talent and Urban Schools," *Phi Delta Kappan*, *81*(5), 304–306; M. S. Knapp, P. M. Shields & B. J. Turnbull (1995), Academic Challenge in High-Poverty Classrooms, "*Phi Delta Kappan*, *76*(10), 770–776; G. Ladson-Billings (1994), *The Dreamkeepers: Successful Teachers of African American Children* (San Francisco: Jossey-Bass); T. Lucas, R. Henze & R. Donato (1990), "Promoting the Success of Latino Language-Minority Students: An Exploratory Study of Six High Schools," *Harvard Educational Review*, *60*(3), 315–340; M. Rose (1995), *Possible Lives: The Promise of Public Education in America* (New York: Penguin Books).

2. S. Nieto (1994), "Lessons From Students on Creating a Chance to Dream," *Harvard Educational Review*, *64*(4), 392–426.

3. A. Portes & R. G. Rumbaut (2001), *Legacies: The Story of the Immigrant Second Generation* (Berkeley: University of California Press and New York: Russell Sage Foundation).

4. See, for instance, E. E. García & A. Hurtado (1995), "Becoming American: A Review of Current Research on the Development of Racial and Ethnic Identity in Children," in W. D. Hawley & A. W. Jackson (eds.), *Toward a Common Destiny: Improving Race and Ethnic Relations in America* (pp. 163–184) (San Francisco: Jossey-Bass); G. Gay (2000), *Culturally Responsive Teaching: Theory, Research, and Practice* (New York: Teachers College Press); and S. Nieto (2000), *Affirming Diversity: The Sociopolitical Context of Multicultural Education*, 3rd ed. (New York: Longman).

5. M. Gibson (1997), "Complicating the Immigrant/Involuntary Minority Typology," *Anthropology and Education Quarterly*, *28*(3), pp. 431–454.

6. S. B. Heath (1983), *Ways With Words* (New York: Cambridge University Press); J. J. Irvine (1990), *Black Students and School Failure: Policies, Practices, and Prescriptions* (Westport, CT: Greenwood Press); G. Ladson-Billings (1994). *The Dreamkeepers: Successful Teachers of African American Children* (San Francisco: Jossey-Bass); and J. Mahiri (1998), *Shooting for Excellence: African American and Youth Culture in New Century Schools* (Urbana, IL: National Council of Teachers of English and New York: Teachers College Press); G. Gay (2000), *Culturally Responsive Teaching: Theory, Research, and Practice* (New York: Teachers College Press.

7. J. Kailin (1999), "How White Teachers Perceive the Problem of Racism in Their Schools: A Case Study of 'Liberal' Lakeview, *Teachers College Record*, *100*(4), 724–750.

8. There is a growing literature on race and racism in schools and the role of White teachers in sustaining it. Among such studies are C. E. Sleeter (1994), "White Racism," *Multicultural Education*, *1*(4), 5–8, 39; K. Jervis (1996), "'How Come There Are No Brothers on That List?': Hearing the Hard Questions All Children Ask," *Harvard Educational Review*, *66*(3), 546–576; A. McIntyre (1997), *Making Meaning of Whiteness: Exploring Racial Identity With White Teachers* (Albany: State University

of New York Press); and G. R. Howard (1999), *"We Can't Teach What We Don't Know": White Teachers, Multiracial Schools* (New York: Teachers College Press).

9. See, for example, N. Noddings (1992), *The Challenge to Care in Schools: An Alternative Approach to Education* (New York: Teachers College Press); A. Valenzuela (1999), *Subtractive Schooling: U.S.-Mexican Youth and the Politics of Caring* (Albany: State University of New York Press).

10. See J. J. Irvine & M. Foster (1996), *Growing Up African American in Catholic Schools* (New York: Teachers College Press); M. Patchen (1982). *Black-White Contact in Schools: Its Social and Academic Effects* (West Lafayette, IN: Purdue University Press); D. Pollard (1989), "A Profile of Underclass Achievers," *Journal of Negro Education, 58,* 297–308; K. Lomotey (1990). *Going to school: The African-American Experience* (Albany: State University of New York Press); and P. U. Treisman (1992), "Studying Students Studying Calculus: A Look at the Lives of Minority Mathematics Students in College," *The College Mathematics Journal, 23*(5), 362–372.

11. J. Bempechat (1999), "Learning from Poor and Minority Students Who Succeed in School," *Harvard Education Letter, 15*(3), 1–3.

12. Ullman J. (1997), *A Case Study of an Urban High School English Class: Encouraging Academic Engagement by Creating a Culture of Respect* (unpublished doctoral dissertation, Boston College, MA), p. 107.

13. J. Oakes, K. H. Quartz, S. Ryan & M. Lipton (2000), *Becoming Good American Schools: The Struggle for Civic Virtue in Education Reform* (San Francisco: Jossey-Bass).

14. N. Zane (1997), "When 'Discipline Problems' Recede: Democracy and Intimacy in Urban Charters," in M. Fine (ed.), *Chartering Urban School Reform: Reflections on Public High Schools in the Midst of Change* (pp. 122–135) (New York: Teachers College Press), p. 128.

15. S. R. Katz (1999), "Teaching in Tensions: Latino Immigrant Youth, Their Teachers, and the Structures of Schooling," *Teachers College Record, 100*(4), 809–840.

16. For more information on teacher research, see M. Cochran-Smith & S. Lytle (1993), *Inside/Outside: Teacher Research and Knowledge* (New York: Teachers College Press); S. W. Freedman, E. R. Simons, J. S. Kalnin, A. Casareno & the M-CLASS Teams (eds.) (1999), *Inside City Schools: Investigating Literacy in Multicultural Classrooms* (New York: Teachers College Press); and J. Kuzmeskus (ed.) (1996), *We Teach Them All: Teachers Writing About Diversity* (York, ME: Stenhouse Publishers).

17. H. Kohl (1994), *"I Won't Learn From You" and Other Thoughts on Creative Maladjustment* (New York: The New Press), p. 76.

18. M. Rose (1989), *Lives on the Boundary* (New York: Penguin).

19. R. L. Fried (1995), *The Passionate Teacher: A Practical Guide* (Boston: Beacon Press), p. 1.

Chapter 4

This chapter was enriched with insights from a group of teachers from English High School: Darryl Alladice, Juan Figueroa, Karen Gelzinis, Anita Preer, Mattie Shields, Patrick Tutwiler (student teacher), and Junia Yearood.

1. M. Greene (1988), *The Dialectic of Freedom* (New York: Teachers College Press), p. 3.

2. J. Dewey (1916), *Democracy and Education* (New York: The Free Press), pp. 119–120.

3. M. B. Katz (1975), *Class, Bureaucracy, and the Schools: The Illusion of Educational Change in America* (New York: Praeger), p. 106.

4. A number of educational historians have explored this matter. See M. Weinberg (1977), *A Chance to Learn: A History of Race and Education in the U.S.* (Cambridge: Cambridge University Press); D. Tyack (1995), "Schooling and Social Diversity: Historical Reflections," in W. D. Hawley & A. W. Jackson (eds.), *Toward a Common Destiny: Improving Race and Ethnic Relations in America* (pp. 3–38) (San Francisco: Jossey-Bass); and J. Spring (2001), *Deculturalization and the Struggle for Equality: A Brief History of the Education of Dominated Cultures in the United States,* 3rd ed. (New York: McGraw-Hill).

5. This echoes one of the major conclusions of a study reported by Marilyn M. Cohn and Robert B. Kottkamp (1993) in *Teachers: The Missing Voice in Education* (Albany: State University of New York Press). The study, conducted between 1964 and 1984, reports on in-depth interviews with 73 teachers and surveys of more than 2,700 teachers.

6. H. Kohl (1994), *"I Won't Learn From You" and Other Thoughts on Creative Maladjustment* (New York: The New Press).

7. P. Freire (1998), *Teachers as Cultural Workers: Letters to Those Who Dare Teach.* (Boulder, CO: Westview Press), p. 3.

Chapter 5

1. This was the case in a study of elementary schools in Tennessee. See S. J. Rosenholtz (1989), *Teachers' Workplace: The Social Organization of Schools* (New York: Longman).

2. For a detailed description of the Massachusetts Reform Act, see D. French (1998), "The State's Role in Shaping a Progressive Vision of Public Education," *Phi Delta Kappan, 80*(3), 185–194.

3. The study that Sister Frances Georgia did is well known. She documented that a huge number of Puerto Rican children were not attending school. Her research was influential in helping to convince the Massachusetts legislature to pass Chapter 71A (1971), the Massachusetts Transitional Bilingual Education Law (TBE), the first law of its kind in the country to mandate bilingual education. It became the model for every other bilingual education law passed in the United States. (See National Coalition of Advocates for Students (1988), *Barriers to Excellence: Our Children at Risk* (Boston: Author).

4. J. Kozol (1967), *Death at an Early Age: The Destruction of the Hearts and Minds of Negro children in the Boston Public Schools* (Boston: Houghton Mifflin).

5. For information on the community-control movement that began in the 1960s, see M. D. Fantini, M. Gittell & R. Magat (1970), *Community Control and the Urban School* (New York: Praeger).

6. For more information on the history of desegregation in Boston in the 1970s, see M. King (1981), *Chain of Change: Struggles for Black Community Development* (Boston: South End Press).

7. T. Sizer & N. Sizer (1999), *The Students Are Watching: Schools and the Moral Contract* (Boston: Beacon Press).

8. A. Hargreaves & M. Fullan (1998), *What's Worth Fighting for Out There?* (New York: Teachers College Press).

9. Marilyn Cohn and Robert Kottkamp (1993), in a study comparing research on teachers in 1964 and 1984, concluded, "The absence of teachers from the dialogue and decision-making on reform has been a serious omission. It has yielded faulty definitions of the problem, solutions that compound rather than confront the problem, and a demeaned and demoralized teaching force" (p. xvi) (M. M. Cohn & R. B. Kottkamp [1993], *Teachers: The Missing Voice in Education*. [Albany: State University of New York Press].

10. In a recent article refuting the critics of teacher education, David Berliner has presented convincing evidence that teachers are as intelligent as lawyers, managers, business executives, and those who work in finance. For the other myths he refutes, see D. C. Berliner (2001), "A Personal Response to Those Who Bash Teacher Education," *Journal of Teacher Education, 51*(5), 358–371. See also L. Darling-Hammond (1997), *Doing What Matters Most: Investing in Teacher Quality* (New York: National Commission on Teaching and America's Future, Teachers College, Columbia University); and D. Gitomer, A. S. Latham & R. Ziomek (1999), *The Academic Quality of Prospective Teachers: The Impact of Admissions and Licensure Testing* (Princeton, NJ: Teaching and Learning Division, Educational Testing Service).

11. The three-part series *Only a Teacher*, directed by Claudia Levin, is a moving tribute to teachers. Through educational history and film clips, and using the words and writings of teachers throughout the years, the film explores many topics, including the feminization of teaching and the subsequent lack of respect for those in the profession. The series is available from Films for the Humanities and Sciences at P.O. Box 2053, Princeton, NJ 08543. The toll-free phone number is (800) 257-5126, and the website is www.films.com.

Chapter 6

1. H. Giroux (1988), *Teachers as Intellectuals: Toward a Critical Pedagogy of Learning* (Granby, MA: Bergin & Garvey), p. xxxiv.

2. M. Cochran-Smith & S. Lytle (1993), *Inside/Outside: Teacher Research and Knowledge* (New York: Teachers College Press), p. 2.

3. B. R. Barber (1992), *An Aristocracy of Everyone: The Politics of Education and the Future of America* (New York: Oxford University Press), p. 229.

4. S. M. Wilson & J. Berne (1999), "Teacher Learning and the Acquisition of Professional Knowledge: An Examination of Research on Contemporary Professional Development, in A. Iran-Nejad & P. D. Pearson (eds.), *Review of Research in Education*, (vol. 24 pp. 173–209) (Washington, DC: American Educational Research Association), p. 181. Further, a recent study by Jane David and Patrick Shields of

seven urban districts found that an investment in extensive professional development over a period of several years is the only reform effort that clearly resulted in student achievement gains (J. L. David & P. M. Shields [2001], *When Theory Hits Reality: Standards-Based Reform in Urban districts, Final Narrative Report* [Menlo Park, CA: SRI International]).

5. An example is a study investigating teachers' understanding of text-based discussion of multiethnic autobiographies, by Susan Florio Ruane and Julie deTar. The researchers found that conversations among teachers were neither simple nor free of conflict. Although discussions were polite, teachers became uncomfortable because they had a hard time finding a way to disagree and critique one another's positions, especially when the subject turned to inequality and racism. When this happened, Florio Ruane and deTar found that the teachers tended to avoid the more difficult discussions. See S. Florio Ruane & J. deTar (1995), "Conflict and consensus in Teacher Candidates' Discussion of Ethnic Autobiography," *English Education, 27*, 11–39.

6. M. Cochran-Smith & S. Lytle (1993), *Inside/Outside: Teacher Research and Knowledge* (New York: Teachers College Press), p. 21.

7. M. Cochran-Smith (1997), "Knowledge, Skills, and Experiences for Teaching Culturally Diverse Learners: A Perspective for Practicing Teachers," In J. J. Irvine (ed.), *Critical Knowledge for Diverse Teachers and Learners* (pp. 27–87) (Washington, DC: American Association of Colleges for Teacher Education).

8. The National Writing Project, for instance, is hugely popular with many teachers, not just with teachers of English, because it affords them the opportunity to write and to work in community. Examples of teacher writing include classics such as *Teacher*, the moving autobiography of a teacher in New Zealand (S. Ashton-Warner (1963), *Teacher* [New York: Simon and Schuster]) and Jonathan Kozol's (1967), *Death at an Early Age: The Destruction of the Hearts and Minds of Negro Children in the Boston Public Schools* (Boston: Houghton Mifflin), to more recent treatments such as William Ayers's (2001), *To Teach: The Journey of a Teacher* (New York: Teachers College Press), Christina Igoa's (1995), *The Inner World of the Immigrant Child* (New York: St. Martins Press); and S. M. Intrator, (ed.) (2002), *Stories of the Courage to Teach: Honoring the Teacher's Heart* (San Francisco: Jossey-Bass). Collaborative efforts include J. Kuzmeskus (1996), *We Teach Them All: Teachers Writing About Diversity* (York, ME: Stenhouse Publishers); and the book by Sara Freedman and her associates (1999), *Inside City Schools: Investigating Literacy in Multicultural Classroom* (New York: Teachers College Press), a book in which contributions from Junia Yearwood and other teachers from around the country were included.

9. Some of the resources that Patty Bode uses in her study of vejigante masks are a video, *The Legend of the Vejigante*, and companion book, *The Vejigante and the Folk Festivals of Puerto Rico*, both by Edwin Fontánez (1995) (Washington, DC: Exit Studio). They are available directly from the artist. The website for Exit Studio is www.exitstudio.com. See also the website for Museo del Barrio (a museum specializing in Puerto Rican arts), www.museo.org. Patty Bode also uses Lulu Delacre's (1993) book, *Vejigante Masquerader* (New York: Scholastic).

10. For a review of the findings of this commission, see L. Darling-Hammond, (1998), "Teachers and Teaching: Testing Policy Hypotheses From a National Com-

mission Report," *Educational Researcher*, 27(2), 5–15, p. 6; See also other recent research that confirms the findings of the Commission: S. Feiman-Nemser (2001), "From Preparation to Practice: Designing a Continuum to Strengthen and Sustain Teaching," *Teachers College Record, 103*(6), 1013–1055; P. Grossman, S. Wineburg & S. Woolworth (2000), *What Makes Teacher Community Different from a Gathering of Teachers?* (Seattle, WA: Center for the Study of Teaching and Policy, and Center for English Learning and Achievement, University of Washington, Seattle); and S. M. Johnson & S. M. Kardos (2002), "Redesigning Professional Development: Keeping New Teachers in Mind." *Educational Leadership, 59*(6), 12–16.

11. T. Raphael (1982), "Question Answering Strategies for Children," *Reading Teacher, 36*(2), 186–190.

12. G. Canada (1995), *Fist, Stick, Knife: A Personal History of Violence in America* (Boston: Beacon Press).

13. P. Freire (1998), *Teachers as Cultural Workers: Letters to Those Who Dare Teach* (Boulder, CO: Westview Press), p. 18.

14. M. Cochran-Smith & S. L. Lytle (1999), "Relationships of Knowledge and Practice: Teacher Learning in Communities, in A. Iran-Nejad & P. D. Pearson (eds.), *Review of Research in Education, 24*, 249–305.

Chapter 7

1. J. Kozol (1991), *Savage Inequalities: Children in America's Schools* (New York: Crown).

2. B. J. Biddle (1997), "Foolishness, Dangerous Nonsense, and Real Correlates of State Differences in Achievement," *Phi Delta Kappan, 79*(1), 9–13.

3. K. Anderson-Levitt (1997), editor's preface, *Anthropology and Education Quarterly, 28*(3), 315–317, 316.

4. F. Cordasco (1973, February), "America and the Quest for Equal Educational Opportunity: The Schools and the Children of the Poor," *British Journal of Educational Studies, 21*, 50–63, p. 63.

5. D. Tyack (1995), "Schooling and Social Diversity: Historical Reflections," in W. D. Hawley & A. W. Jackson (eds.), *Toward a Common Destiny: Improving Race and Ethnic Relations in America* (pp. 3–38) (San Francisco: Jossey-Bass), p. 4.

6. J. Oakes, K. H. Quartz, S. Ryan & M. Lipton (2000), *Becoming Good American Schools: The Struggle for Civic Virtue in Education Reform* (San Francisco: Jossey-Bass).

7. See, for example, L. Darling-Hammond (1996), The Right to Learn and the Advancement of Teaching: Research, Policy, and Practice for Democratic Education. *Educational Researcher, 25*(6), 5–17.

8. T. Sizer (1984), *Horace's Compromise: The Dilemma of the American High School* (Boston: Houghton Mifflin), p. 6.

9. E. Hanssen (1998), "A White Teacher Reflects on Institutional Racism," *Phi Delta Kappan, 79*(9), 694–698, p. 698.

10. A. H. Lima (2000), "Voices From the Basement: Breaking Through the Pedagogy of Indifference," in Z. F. Beykont (ed.), *Lifting Every Voice: Pedagogy and Politics of Bilingualism* (pp. 221–232) (Cambridge, MA: Harvard Education Publishing Group), p. 222.

11. P. Freire (1998), *Teachers as Cultural Workers: Letters to Those Who Dare Teach* (Boulder, CO: Westview Press).

12. V. Perrone (1991), *A Letter to Teachers: Reflections on Schooling and the Art of Teaching* (San Francisco: Jossey-Bass).

13. Two books that challenge traditional history are J. Loewen (1995), *Lies My Teacher Told Me: Everything Your American History Textbook Got Wrong* (New York: New Press); and H. Zinn (1980), *A People's History of the United States* (New York: Harper & Row). Books and other resources that describe what happens when these perspectives are brought into the classroom are H. Levin (1998), *Teach Me! Kids Will Learn When Oppression Is the Lesson* (Lanham, MD: Rowman & Littlefield) and any of the Rethinking Schools publications (all written by teachers), including the two volumes of *Rethinking Our Classrooms* (Milwaukee, WI: Rethinking Schools). A book that describes excellent community-building strategies for the classroom is N. Schniedewind & E. Davidson (1998), *Open Minds to Equality: A Sourcebook of Learning Activities to Affirm Diversity and Promote Equity* (Boston: Allyn & Bacon).

14. D. Cronin (2000), *Click, Clack, Moo: Cows That Type* (New York: Scholastic).

15. D. Macaulay (1988). *The Way Things Work* (London: Dorling Kindersly).

Chapter 8

1. National Education Association (1997), *Status of the American Public School Teacher* (Washington, DC: Author).

2. For various perspectives on small schools, see W. Ayers (ed.) (2000), *Simple Justice: The Small Schools Revolution and the Fight for Fairness in Our Schools* (New York: Teachers College Press), pp. 13–17.

3. L. Olsen (1988), *Crossing the Schoolhouse Border: Immigrant Students and the California Public Schools* (San Francisco: California Tomorrow). For other examples, see S. Nieto (1994), "Lessons from Students on Creating a Chance to Dream," *Harvard Educational Review*, 64(4), 392–426.

4. E. Fraser, "Words That Kill," *Message Magazine*, pp. 4–5, 4.

5. D. Gregory, with R. Lipsyte (1964), *Nigger: An Autobiography* (New York: Dutton).

6. M. Rose (1989), *Lives on the Boundary* (New York: Penguin).

7. M. Angelou (1969), *I Know Why the Caged Bird Sings* (New York: Random House).

Chapter 9

1. M. W. McLaughlin & J. E. Talbert (2001), *Professional Communities and the Work of High School Teaching* (Chicago: University of Chicago Press).

2. D. C. Lortie (1975), *Schoolteacher: A Sociological Study* (Chicago: University of Chicago Press).

3. For an extensive review of teacher learning, see M. Cochran-Smith & S. L. Lytle (1999), "Relationships of Knowledge and Practice: Teacher Learning in Communities," in A. Iran-Nejad, & P. D. Pearson (eds.), *Review of Research in Edu-

cation, 24, pp. 249–305. See also M. K. Stein, M. S. Smith & E. A. Silver (1999), "The Development of Professional Educators: Learning to Assist Teachers in New Settings in New Ways," *Harvard Educational Review, 69*(3), 237–269.

4. See notes 11 and 12 in the Introduction.

5. See, for instance, M. Fullan (2000), "The Three Stories of Education Reform," *Phi Delta Kappan, 81*(8), 581–584; L. Darling-Hammond (1997), *The Right to Learn: A Blueprint for Creating Schools That Work* (San Francisco: Jossey-Bass); and J. W. Little (1991), "Organizing Schools for Teacher Learning," in L. Darling-Hammond & G. Sykes (eds.), *Teaching as the Learning Profession: Handbook of Policy and Practice* (pp. 233–262) (San Francisco; Jossey-Bass).

6. R. M. Ingersoll (2001), "Teacher Turnover and Teacher Shortages: An Organizational Analysis," *American Educational Research Journal, 38*(3), 499–534. See also M. Schmoker (2002), "Up and Away: The Formula is Well-Known, Now We Need to Follow It," *Journal of Staff Development, 23*(2), 10–13.

7. D. Viadero (2001, November 7), "Whole-School Projects Show Mixed Results," *Education Week, 21*(10), 1.

References

Anderson-Levitt, K. (1997). Editor's preface. *Anthropology and Education Quarterly, 28*(3), 315–317.

Angelou, M. (1969). *I know why the caged bird sings.* New York: Random House.

Ashton-Warner, S. (1963). *Teacher.* New York: Simon and Schuster.

Ayers, W. (Ed.). (2000). *A simple justice: The challenge of small schools.* New York: Teachers College Press.

Ayers, W. (2001). *To teach: The journey of a teacher* (2nd ed.). New York: Teachers College Press.

Banks, J. A. (Ed.). (1973). *Teaching ethnic studies: Concepts and strategies.* 43rd Yearbook. Washington, DC: National Council for the Social Studies.

Barber, B. R. (1992). *An aristocracy of everyone: The politics of education and the future of America.* New York: Oxford University Press.

Bempechat, J. (1999). Learning from poor and minority students who succeed in school. *Harvard Education Letter, 15*(3), 1–3.

Berliner, D. C. (2001). A personal response to those who bash teacher education. *Journal of Teacher Education, 51*(5), 358–371.

Biddle, B. J. (1997). Foolishness, dangerous nonsense, and real correlates of state differences in achievement. *Phi Delta Kappan, 79*(1), 9–13.

Bowles, S., & Gintis, H. (1976). *Schooling in capitalist America: Educational reform and the contradictions of economic life.* New York: Basic Books.

Bruner, J. S. (1983). *In search of mind: Essays in autobiography.* New York: Harper & Row.

Bruner, J. S. (1994). Life as narrative. In A. H. Dyson & C. Genishi (Eds.), *The need for story: Cultural diversity in classroom and community* (pp. 28–37). Urbana, IL: National Council of Teachers of English.

Buckley, S. (2000, February 2). Root of all evil: Money makes the sports world go round. *Boston Herald,* p. 102.

Campuzano, B. (2001). A better chance. *Narratives, 6*(1), 25–26.

Canada, G. (1995). *Fist, stick, knife: A personal history of violence in America.* Boston: Beacon Press.

Casey, K. (1993). *I answer with my life: Life histories of women teachers working for social change.* New York: Routledge.

Clanindin, D. J., Davies, A., Hogan, P., & Kennard, B. (1993). *Learning to teach, teaching to learn: Stories of collaboration in teacher education.* New York: Teachers College Press.

Clewell, B. C., Puma, M., & McKay, S. A. (2001). *Does it matter if my teacher looks like me?: The impact of teacher race and ethnicity on student academic achievement.* New York: Ford Foundation.

Cochran-Smith, M. (1997). Knowledge, skills, and experiences for teaching culturally diverse learners: A perspective for practicing teachers. In J. J. Irvine (Ed.), *Critical knowledge for diverse teachers and learners* (pp. 27–87). Washington, DC: American Association of Colleges for Teacher Education.

Cochran-Smith, M. (2000). Blind vision: Unlearning racism in teacher education. *Harvard Educational Review, 70*(2), 157–190.

Cochran-Smith, M., & Lytle, S. (1993). *Inside/outside: Teacher research and knowledge.* New York: Teachers College Press.

Cochran-Smith, M., & Lytle, S. L. (1999). Relationships of knowledge and practice: Teacher learning in communities. In A. Iran-Nejad & P. David Pearson (Eds.), *Review of research in education, 24,* 249–305.

Cohen, R. M., & Scheer, S. (Eds.). (1997). *The work of teachers in America: A social history through stories.* New York: Longman.

Cohn, M. M., & Kottkamp, R. B. (1993). *Teachers: The missing voice in education.* Albany: State University of New York Press.

Connelly, F. M., & Clandinin, D. J. (1999). *Shaping a professional identity: Stories of educational practice.* New York: Teachers College Press.

Cordasco, F. (1973, February). America and the quest for equal educational opportunity: The schools and the children of the poor. *British Journal of Educational Studies, 21,* 50–63.

Darling-Hammond, L. (1996). The right to learn and the advancement of teaching: Research, policy, and practice for democratic education. *Educational Researcher, 25*(6), 5–17.

Darling-Hammond, L. (1997). *Doing what matters most: Investing in teacher quality.* New York: National Commission on Teaching and America's Future, Teachers College, Columbia University.

Darling-Hammond, L. (1997). *The right to learn: A blueprint for creating schools that work.* San Francisco: Jossey-Bass.

Darling-Hammond, L. (1998). Teachers and teaching: Testing policy hypotheses from a National Commission Report. *Educational Researcher, 27*(2), 5–15.

Darling-Hammond, L., & Falk, B. (1997). Using standards and assessments to support student learning. *Phi Delta Kappan, 79*(3), 190–199.

David, J. L., & Shields, P. M. (2001). *When theory hits reality: Standards-based reform in urban districts, final narrative report.* Menlo Park, CA: SRI International.

Dee, T. S. (2000). *Teachers, race, and student achievement in a randomized experiment.* Cambridge, MA: National Bureau of Economic Research.

Delacre, L. (1993). *Vejigante Masquerador.* New York: Scholastic.

Delpit, L. D. (1988). The silenced dialogue: Power and pedagogy in educating other people's children. *Harvard Educational Review, 58,* 280–298.

Dewey, J. (1916). *Democracy and education.* New York: The Free Press.

Dickeman, M. (1973). Teaching cultural pluralism. In J. A. Banks (Ed.), *Teaching ethnic studies: Concepts and strategies* (pp. 4–25). 43rd Yearbook. Washington, DC: National Council for the Social Studies.

Dominicé, P. (2000). *Learning from our lives: Using educational biographies with adults.* San Francisco: Jossey-Bass.

Education Commission of the States. (2000). *In pursuit of quality teaching: Five key strategies for policymakers*. Denver, CO: Education Commission of the States.

Fantini, M. D., Gittell, M., & Magat, R. (1970). *Community control and the urban school*. New York: Praeger Publishers.

Farkas, S., Johnson, J., & Foleno, T. (2000). *A sense of calling: Who teaches and why*. New York: Public Agenda.

Feiman-Nemser, S. (2001). From preparation to practice: Designing a continuum to strengthen and sustain teaching. *Teachers College Record, 103*(6), 1013–1055.

Florio Ruane, S., & deTar, J. (1995). Conflict and consensus in teacher candidates' discussion of ethnic autobiography. *English Education, 27*, 11–39.

Fontánez, E. (1995). *The Vejigante and the folk festivals of Puerto Rico*. Washington, DC: Exit Studios

Fox, R. F. (Ed.). (2000). *Case studies in teacher renewal*. Urbana, IL: National Council of Teachers of English.

Fraser, E. (DATE??). Words that kill. *Message Magazine*, pp. 4–5.

Freedman, S. W., Simons, E. R., Kalnin, J. S., Casareno, A., & the M-CLASS Teams (Eds.). (1999). *Inside city schools: Investigating literacy in multicultural classrooms*. New York: Teachers College Press.

Freire, P. (1970). *Pedagogy of the oppressed*. New York: Seabury Press.

Freire, P. (1998). *Teachers as cultural workers: Letters to those who dare teach*. Boulder, CO: Westview Press.

French, D. (1998). The state's role in shaping a progressive vision of public education. *Phi Delta Kappan, 80*(3), 185–194.

Fried, R. L. (1995). *The passionate teacher: A practical guide*. Boston: Beacon Press

Fullan, M. (2000). The three stories of education reform. *Phi Delta Kappan, 81*(8), 581–584.

García, E. E. (1999). *Student cultural diversity: Understanding and meeting the challenge* (2nd ed.). Boston: Houghton Mifflin.

García, E. E., & Hurtado, A. (1995). Becoming American: A review of current research on the development of racial and ethnic identity in children. In W. D. Hawley & A. W. Jackson (Eds.), *Toward a common destiny: Improving race and ethnic relations in America* (pp. 163–184). San Francisco: Jossey-Bass.

Gay, G. (2000). *Culturally responsive teaching: Theory, research, and practice*. New York: Teachers College Press.

Gibson, L. (1998). Teaching as an encounter with the self: Unraveling the mix of personal beliefs, education ideologies, and pedagogical practices. *Anthropology and Education Quarterly, 29*(3), 360–371.

Gibson, M. (1997). Complicating the immigrant/involuntary minority typology. *Anthropology and Education Quarterly, 28*(3), 431–454.

Giroux, H. A. (1988). *Teachers as intellectuals: Toward a critical pedagogy of learning*. Granby, MA: Bergin & Garvey.

Gitomer, D., Latham, A. S., & Ziomek, R. (1999). *The academic quality of prospective teachers: The impact of admissions and licensure testing*. Princeton, NJ: Teaching and Learning Division, Educational Testing Service.

Gordon, G. (1999). Teacher talent and urban schools. *Phi Delta Kappan, 81*(5), 304–306.

Greene, M. (1978). *Landscapes of learning.* New York: Teachers College Press.

Greene, M. (1988). *The dialectic of freedom.* New York: Teachers College Press.

Greene, M. (1991). Foreword. In C. Witherell & N. Noddings (Eds.), *Stories lives tell: Narrative and dialogue in education.* New York: Teachers College Press.

Grossman, P., Wineburg, S., & Woolworth, S. (2000). *What makes teacher community different from a gathering of teachers?* Seattle, WA: Center for the Study of Teaching and Policy, and Center for English Learning and Achievement, University of Washington, Seattle.

Haberman, M. (1988). *Preparing teachers for urban schools.* Bloomington, IN: Phi Delta Kappa Educational Foundation.

Hanssen, E. (1998). A White teacher reflects on institutional racism. *Phi Delta Kappan, 79*(9), 694–698.

Hargreaves, A., Earl, L., & Ryan, J. (1996). *Schooling for change.* New York: Falmer Press.

Hargreaves, A., & Fullan, M. (1998). *What's worth fighting for out there?* New York: Teachers College Press.

Haycock, K. (1998). Good teaching matters. *Thinking K–16, 3*(2), 1–2.

Heath, S. B. (1983). *Ways with words.* New York: Cambridge University Press.

Helfand, D. (2001, December 12). Lack of qualified teachers undermines state reforms. *Los Angeles Times,* [Online]. Available: www.latimes.com/news/local/la-0000986.50dec12.story?coll=la%2Dcalifornia.

Henke, R. R., Chen, X., & Geis, S. (2000). *Progress through the teacher pipeline: College graduates and elementary/secondary school teaching as of 1997.* Washington, DC: National Center for Education Statistics.

Henke, R. R., Choy, S. P., Chen, X., Geis, S., & Alt, M. N. (1997). *America's teachers: Profile of a profession, 1993–94, NCES 97–460.* Washington, DC: United States Department of Education.

hooks, b. (1994). *Teaching to transgress: Education as the practice of freedom.* New York: Routledge.

Howard, G. R. (1999). *We can't teach what we don't know: White teachers, multiracial schools.* New York: Teachers College Press.

Hussar, W. J. (1999). *Predicting the need for newly hired teachers in the United States to 2008–2009.* Washington, DC: National Center for Education Statistics.

Igoa, C. (1995). *The inner world of the immigrant child.* New York: St. Martins Press.

Ingersoll, R. M. (2001). Teacher turnover and teacher shortages: An organizational analysis. *American Educational Research Journal, 38*(3), 499–534.

Intrator, S. M. (Ed.). (2002). *Stories of the courage to teach: Honoring the teacher's heart.* San Francisco: Jossey-Bass.

Irvine, J. J. (1990). *Black students and school failure: Policies, practices, and prescriptions.* Westport, CT: Greenwood Press.

Irvine, J. J., & Foster, M. (1996). *Growing up African American in Catholic schools.* New York: Teachers College Press.

Jervis, K. (1996). "How come there are no brothers on that list?": Hearing the hard questions all children ask. *Harvard Educational Review, 66*(3), 546–576.

Johnson, S. M. (1990). *Teachers at work: Achieving success in our schools.* New York: Basic Books.

Johnson, S. M., & Kardos, S. M. (2002). Redesigning professional development: Keeping new teachers in mind. *Educational Leadership, 59*(6), 12–16.

Kailin, J. (1999). How White teachers perceive the problem of racism in their schools: A case study of "liberal" Lakeview. *Teachers College Record, 100*(4), 724–750.

Katz, M. B. (1975). *Class, bureaucracy, and the schools: The illusion of educational change in America.* New York: Praeger.

Katz, S. R. (1999). Teaching in tensions: Latino immigrant youth, their teachers, and the structures of schooling. *Teachers College Record, 100*(4), 809–840.

King, M. (1981). *Chain of change: Struggles for Black community development.* Boston: South End Press.

Knapp, M. S., Shields, P. M., & Turnbull, B. J. (1995). Academic challenge in high-poverty classrooms. *Phi Delta Kappan, 76*(10), 770–776.

Kohl, H. (1967). *36 Children.* New York: New American Library.

Kohl, H. (1994). *"I won't learn from you" and other thoughts on creative maladjustment.* New York: The New Press.

Kozol, J. (1967). *Death at an early age: The destruction of the hearts and minds of Negro children in the Boston Public Schools.* Boston: Houghton Mifflin.

Kozol, J. (1991). *Savage inequalities: Children in America's schools.* New York: Crown.

Kuzmeskus, J. (Ed.). (1996). *We teach them all: Teachers writing about diversity.* York, ME: Stenhouse.

Ladson-Billings, G. (1994). *The dreamkeepers: Successful teachers of African American children.* San Francisco: Jossey-Bass.

Langdon, C. A., & Vesper, N. (2000). The sixth Phi Delta Kappa Poll of teachers' attitudes toward the public schools. *Phi Delta Kappan, 81*(8), 607–611.

Langer, J. (2002). Beating the odds: Teaching middle and high school students to read and write well. *American Educational Research Journal, 38*(4), 837–880.

Levin, M. (1998). *Teach me!: Kids will learn when oppression is the lesson.* Lanham, MD: Rowman & Littlefield.

Lima, A. H. (2000). Voices from the basement: Breaking through the pedagogy of indifference. In Z. F. Beykont (Ed.), *Lifting every voice: Pedagogy and politics of bilingualism* (pp. 221–232). Cambridge, MA: Harvard Education Publishing Group.

Little, J. W. (1991). Organizing schools for teacher learning. In L. Darling-Hammond & G. Sykes (Eds.), *Teaching as the learning profession: Handbook of policy and practice* (pp. 233–262). San Francisco: Jossey-Bass.

Loewen, J. W. (1995). *Lies my teacher told me: Everything your American history textbook got wrong.* New York: New Press.

Lomotey, K. (1990). *Going to school: The African-American experience.* Albany: State University of New York Press

Lucas, T., Henze, R., & Donato, R. (1990). Promoting the success of Latino language-minority students: An exploratory study of six high schools. *Harvard Educational Review, 60*(3), 315–340;

Mahiri, J. (1998). *Shooting for excellence: African American and youth culture in new century schools.* Urbana, IL: National Council of Teachers of English; New York: Teachers College Press.

McIntyre, A. (1997). *Making meaning of Whiteness: Exploring racial identity with White teachers.* Albany: State University of New York Press.

McLaughlin, M. W., & Talbert, J. E. (2001). *Professional communities and the work of high school teaching.* Chicago: University of Chicago Press.

Meier, K. J., Wrinkle, R. D., & Polinard, J. L. (1999). Representative bureaucracy and distributional equity: Addressing the hard question. *Journal of Politics, 61,* 1025–1039.

Miller, J. L. (1978, May). *An interview with Maxine Greene* [Videotape]. The Curriculum Collection, Museum of Education, University of South Carolina, Columbia.

National Center for Education Statistics. (2000). *Digest of education statistics, 1999.* Washington, DC: Author.

National Center for Education Statistics (2000). *Editorial projects in education, 1998.* Washington, DC: Author.

National Coalition of Advocates for Students. (1988). *Barriers to excellence: Our children at risk.* Boston: Author.

National Commission on Teaching and America's Future. (1996). *What matters most: Teaching for America's future.* New York: Author.

National Education Association. (1997). *Status of the American public school teacher.* Washington, DC: Author.

Nieto, S. (1994). Lessons from students on creating a chance to dream. *Harvard Educational Review, 64*(4), 392–426.

Nieto, S. (1995). From brown heroes and holidays to assimilationist agendas: Reconsidering the critiques of multicultural education. In C. E. Sleeter & P. McLaren (Eds.), *Multicultural education, Critical pedagogy, and the politics of difference* (pp. 191–220). Albany: State University of New York Press.

Nieto, S. (1999). *The light in their eyes: Creating multicultural learning communities.* New York: Teachers College Press.

Nieto, S. (2000). *Affirming diversity: The sociopolitical context of multicultural education,* 3rd ed. New York: Longman (1st ed.: 1992)

Noblitt, G. W. (1993). Power and caring. *American Educational Research Journal, 3*(1), 23–38.

Noddings, N. (1992). *The challenge to care in schools: An alternative approach to education.* New York: Teachers College Press.

Oakes, J., Quartz, K. H., Ryan, S., & Lipton, M. (2000). *Becoming good American schools: The struggle for civic virtue in education reform.* San Francisco: Jossey-Bass.

Olsen, L. (1988). *Crossing the schoolhouse border: Immigrant students and the California public schools.* San Francisco: California Tomorrow.

Orfield, G. & Yun, J. T. (1999, June). *Resegregation in American schools.* Cambridge, MA: Civil Rights Project at Harvard University.

Patchen, M. (1982). *Black-White contact in schools: Its social and academic effects.* West Lafayette, IN: Purdue University Press.

Perrone, V. (1991). *A letter to teachers: Reflections on schooling and the art of teaching.* San Francisco: Jossey-Bass.

Pollard, D. (1989). A profile of underclass achievers. *Journal of Negro Education, 58,* 297–308.

Portes, A. & Rumbaut, R. G. (2001). *Legacies: The story of the immigrant second generation.* Berkeley: University of California Press and New York: Russell Sage Foundation.

Public Education Network and *Education Week.* (2001, April). *Action for all: The public's responsibility for public education.* Washington, DC: Authors.

Raphael, T. (1982). Question answering strategies for children. *Reading Teacher, 36*(2), 186–190.

Rose, M. (1989). *Lives on the boundary.* New York: Penguin.

Rose, M. (1995). *Possible lives: The promise of public education in America.* New York: Penguin Books.

Rosenholtz, S. J. (1989). *Teachers' workplace: The social organization of schools.* New York: Longman.

Schmoker, M. (2002). Up and away: The formula is well-known, now we need to follow it. *Journal of Staff Development, 23*(2), 10–13.

Schniedewind, N., & Davidson, E. (1998). *Open minds to equality: A sourcebook of learning activities to affirm diversity and promote equity.* Boston: Allyn & Bacon.

Shin, P. H. B. (2001, June 19). Teachers are key to success: It's sink or swim for class rookies. *New York Daily News* [Online]. Available: http://www.nydailynews.com/City_Beat/a-115421.asp.

Shor, I., & Freire, P. (1987). *A pedagogy for liberation: Dialogues on transforming education.* New York: Bergin & Garvey.

Sizer, T. (1984). *Horace's compromise: The dilemma of the American high school.* Boston: Houghton Mifflin.

Sizer, T., & Sizer, N. F. (1999). *The students are watching: Schools and the moral contract.* Boston: Beacon Press.

Sleeter, C. E. (1994). White racism. *Multicultural Education, 1*(4), 5–8, 39.

Sleeter, C. (2001). An analysis of the critiques of multicultural education. In J. A. Banks & C. A. M. Banks (Eds.), *Handbook of research on multicultural education* (pp. 81–94). San Francisco: Jossey-Bass.

Snyder, T. D., & Hoffman, C. N. (2002). *Digest of Education Statistics, 2001.* Washington, DC: National Center for Education Statistics.

Spring, J. (2001). *Deculturalization and the struggle for equality: A brief history of the education of dominated cultures in the United States,* 3rd ed. New York: McGraw-Hill.

Stein, M. K., Smith, M. S., & Silver, E. A. (1999). The development of professional educators: Learning to assist teachers in new settings in new ways. *Harvard Educational Review, 69*(3), 237–269.

Stinnett, T. M. (Ed.). (1970). *The teacher dropout.* Bloomington, IN: Phi Delta Kappan.

Stotsky, S. (1999). *Losing our language: How multicultural classroom instruction is undermining our children's ability to read, write, and reason.* New York: The Free Press.

Treisman, P. U. (1992). Studying students studying calculus: A look at the lives of minority mathematics students in college. *The College Mathematics Journal,* 23(5), 362–372.

Tyack, D. (1995). Schooling and social diversity: Historical reflections. In W. D. Hawley & A. W. Jackson (Eds.), *Toward a common destiny: Improving race and ethnic relations in America* (pp. 3–38). San Francisco: Jossey-Bass.

Ullman, J. (1997). *A case study of an urban high school English class: Encouraging academic engagement by creating a culture of respect.* Unpublished doctoral dissertation, Boston College, MA.

United States Bureau of the Census. (2000). *Statistical Abstract of the United States* [Online]. Available: http://www.census.gov/prod/www/statistical-abstract-us.html.

Valenzuela, A. (1999). *Subtractive schooling: U.S.-Mexican youth and the politics of caring.* Albany: State University of New York Press.

Vegas, E., Murname, R. J., & Willett, J. B. (2001). From high school to teaching: Many steps, who makes it? *Teachers College Record, 103*(3), 427–449.

Viadero, D. (2001). Whole-school projects show mixed results. *Education Week, 21*(10), 1, 24–25.

Wadsworth, D. (2001). Why new teachers choose to teach. *Educational Leadership, 58*(8), 24–28.

Weinberg, M. (1977). *A chance to learn: A history of race and education in the U.S.* Cambridge: Cambridge University Press.

Wilson, S. M., & Berne, J. (1999). Teacher learning and the acquisition of professional knowledge: An examination of research on contemporary professional development. In A. Iran-Nejad & P. D. Pearson (Eds.), *Review of research in education,* (vol. 24, pp. 173–209). Washington, DC: American Educational Research Association.

Witherell, C., & Noddings, N. (Eds.). (1991). *Stories lives tell: Narrative and dialogue in education.* New York: Teachers College Press.

Zane, N. (1997). When "discipline problems" recede: Democracy and intimacy in urban charters. In M. Fine (Ed.), *Chartering urban school reform: Reflections on public high schools in the midst of change* (pp. 122–135). New York: Teachers College Press.

Index

Affirming Diversity (Nieto), 18–19, 107
African Americans
  culture of power and, 29
  resegregation of schools and, 4
  as teachers, 2–3, 29–30
Alienation, 5
Alladice, Darryl, 54, 55, 58, 60
Alt, M. N., 132 n. 10
Anderson-Levitt, Kathryn, 93, 141 n. 3
Angelou, Maya, 24, 29, 111, 142 n. 7
Anger of teachers, 63–75
  bureaucratic restructuring and, 65–69
  desperation and, 72–73
  lack of respect and, 71–72
  moving beyond, 73–74
  nature of, 63–65
  school system and, 69–70
Aristotle, 63
Art curriculum, 81–86
Ashton-Warner, Sylvia, 18, 134 n. 5, 140 n. 8
Assimilation
  historical amnesia and, 25
  premature, 40–41
Ayers, William, 9, 140 n. 8, 142 n. 2

Baker, Judith, 42–47, 51, 74, 89, 90
Banks, C. A. M., 134 n. 3
Banks, James A., 18, 134 n. 3, 134 n. 5, 135 n. 6
Barber, Benjamin R., 78, 139 n. 3
Bell, Claudia, 31–32, 47–49, 51, 123–124
Bempechat, Janine, 43, 137 n. 11
Berliner, David C., 139 n. 10
Berne, Jennifer, 78, 139–140 n. 4

"Best practices", in teaching, 125, 128
Beykont, Z. F., 141 n. 10
Biculturalism, 13–14
Biddle, B. J., 141 n. 2
Bilingual education
  Brooklyn College teacher preparation program, 15–16
  PS 25 (Bilingual School; Brooklyn, New York), 12–15
Black Panthers, 13
Blacks. *See* African Americans
Bode, Patty, 77, 81–86, 122–123, 140 n. 9
Boston Herald, 23, 34–36
Bowles, Samuel, 18, 134 n. 4
Brooklyn College, bilingual education teacher preparation program, 15–16
Bruner, Jerome S., 25, 135 n. 4, 135 n. 5
Buckley, Steve, 34, 135 n. 1

Campuzano, Beatriz, 20–21, 135 n. 10
Canada, Geoffrey, 86–87, 88, 141 n. 12
Caring, 2, 29, 37–52
  anger of teachers and, 63–75
  educational reform and, 47–49
  effective teaching and, 38–39
  fundamental belief in students and, 51–52
  hope and, 53–62
  nature of, 42–43
  personal connection and, 43–49
  student identity and, 20–21, 39–42
  teaching metaphors and, 49–51
Casareno, A., 133–134 n. 24, 137 n. 16
Casey, K., 133–134 n. 24

Chen, X., 132 n. 10, 132 n. 13
Child-centered education, 28–29
Choice of education, 5
Choy, S. P., 132 n. 10
Christopher Gibson School (Boston), 67–68
Civil rights movement, 13, 16–17, 23–24, 94
Clandinin, D. J., 133–134 n. 24, 135 n. 4
Clewell, B. C., 132 n. 11
Climate, of schools, 4, 9, 47
Cochran-Smith, Marilyn, 77, 79, 133–134 n. 24, 135 n. 7, 137 n. 16, 139 n. 2, 140 n. 6, 140 n. 7, 141 n. 14, 142–143 n. 3
Cohen, R. M., 135 n. 4
Cohn, Marilyn M., 138 n. 5, 139 n. 9
Community
  importance of, 121–122, 124
  sustaining, 77–79, 90
Connelly, F. M., 135 n. 4
Cordasco, Francesco, 93–94, 141 n. 4
Cortés, Carlos, 18
Cowhey, Mary, 92, 100–106, 122–123
Cronin, D., 142 n. 14
Culture of power, 29
Curriculum
  in multicultural education, 11–12
  nature of, 11
  power of, 11–12
  writing in development of, 81–89

Daly, Ceronne, 112
Darling-Hammond, Linda, 131–132 nn. 4–5, 139 n. 10, 140–141 n. 10, 141 n. 7, 143 n. 5
David, Jane L., 131 n. 4, 139–140 n. 4
Davidson, E., 142 n. 13
Davies, A., 133–134 n. 24
Death at an Early Age (Kozol), 67–68
Dee, T. S., 132 n. 11
Delacre, Lulu, 140 n. 9
Delpit, Lisa D., 29, 99, 135 n. 11
Democratic society, 5, 99–105, 123. See also Social justice

DeTar, Julie, 140 n. 5
Dewey, John, 9, 54, 138 n. 2
Dialectic of Freedom, The (Greene), 53
Dialogue
  Socratic, 11
  between teachers, 77–79
Dickeman, Mildred, 25, 135 n. 6
Discipline, 10–11, 47
Dominicé, Pierre, 22, 135 n. 4
Donato, R., 136 n. 1
Dropouts
  student, 15, 19
  teacher, 3–4, 10, 132–133 n. 14
Dyson, A. H., 135 n. 5

Earl, L., 132 n. 7
Economic privilege, 18–19
Educational reform, 5
  caring and, 47–49
Effective teaching
  caring and, 38–39. See also Caring
  as intellectual work, 76–90, 122–123, 126–127
Equity in education
  economic privilege and, 2, 18–19, 92–94
  lack of, 14–15
  racism and, 4–5, 6, 17, 25, 41, 92, 94–96, 136–137 n. 8
  struggle for, 92–94

Falk, Beverly, 131–132 n. 5
Fantini, M. D., 138 n. 5
Farkas, S., 133 n. 21
Feiman-Nemser, S., 140–141 n. 10
Felix, Sonie, 37, 45, 56–57, 69, 72–75, 112, 114–119
Figueroa, Juan, 41–42, 54, 55–56
Fine, M., 137 n. 14
Fist Stick Gun Knife (Canada), 86–87, 88
Florio Ruane, Susan, 140 n. 5
Foleno, T., 133 n. 21
Font nez, Edwin, 140 n. 9
Foster, M., 137 n. 10
Fox, R. F., 133–134 n. 24
Fraser, Edith, 109, 142 n. 4

Freedman, Sara W., 133–134 n. 24, 137
    n. 16, 140 n. 8
Freire, Paolo, 15, 18–19, 61, 87, 91, 96,
    99, 102, 115–116, 134 nn. 1–2, 134
    n. 5, 135 n. 8, 138 n. 7, 141 n. 13,
    142 n. 11
French, D., 138 n. 2
Fried, Robert L., 51–52, 137 n. 19
Frost, Robert, 28
Fullan, Michael, 53, 139 n. 8, 143 n. 5

García, E. E., 136 n. 1, 136 n. 4
Gay, Geneva, 18, 136 n. 4, 136 n. 6
Gee, James, 99
Geis, S., 132 n. 10, 132 n. 13
Gelzinis, Karen, 41–42, 48, 53, 55, 58–
    59, 61, 64, 66–70, 71, 72, 74, 90,
    108, 111–119, 126
Genishi, C., 135 n. 5
Georgia, Frances, 138 n. 3
Gerould, Kim, 103
Gibson, Linda, 25, 135 n. 3
Gibson, Margaret, 40–41, 136 n. 5
Gintis, Herbert, 18, 134 n. 4
Giroux, Henry, 76, 139 n. 1
Gitomer, D., 139 n. 10
Gittell, M., 138 n. 5
Gomes, Manuel, 107
Gordon, G., 136 n. 1
Gordon, Stephen, 30–31, 37, 51, 65, 66,
    77–78, 79–81, 86–89, 90, 92, 97–99,
    105–106, 122–123, 125, 127
Grant, Carol, 18
Greene, Maxine, 18, 29, 53, 134 n. 5,
    138 n. 1
Gregory, Dick, 110, 142 n. 5
Grossman, P., 140–141 n. 10
Gulley, Andrew P., 34–35

Haberman, M., 133 n. 15, 136 n. 1
Hanssen, Evelyn, 95, 141 n. 9
Hargreaves, Andy, 53, 132 n. 7, 139
    n. 8
Hawley, W. D., 136 n. 4, 138 n. 4, 141
    n. 5
Haycock, Kati, 2, 132 n. 6, 133 n. 15

Heath, S. B., 136 n. 6
Helfand, D., 131 n. 4
Henke, R. R., 132 n. 10, 132 n. 13
Henze, R., 136 n. 1
High-stakes tests, 2, 5
Hispanic Americans
    Brooklyn College bilingual teacher
        preparation program, 15–16
    PS 25 (Bilingual School, Bronx, New
        York), 12–15
    resegregation of schools and, 4
    as teachers, 2–3
Hoffman, C. M., 132 n. 10
Hogan, P., 133–134 n. 24
Home visits, 10, 11
hooks, bell, 37, 135 n. 2
Hope, 53–62
    as catalyst for courage, 61–62
    confidence in colleagues, 58–61
    faith in abilities as teachers, 58
    and promise of public education,
        54–57
Howard, G. R., 136–137 n. 8
Hurtado, A., 136 n. 4
Hussar, W. J., 133 n. 17

Igoa, Christina, 140 n. 8
I Know Why the Caged Bird Sings
    (Angelou), 24
Ingersoll, Richard M., 133 n. 16, 143
    n. 6
Innovations in education, 14
Institutional racism, 95–96
Intellectual work of teaching, 76–90,
    122–123, 126–127
    curriculum development and, 81–89
    need for adult conversations, 77–79
    research in, 76–77, 87
    sustaining community and, 77–79,
        90
    writing and, 79–89
International Reading Association
    (IRA), 99
Intrator, S. M., 133–134 n. 24, 140 n. 8
Iran-Nejad, A., 139–140 n. 4, 141 n. 14,
    142–143 n. 3

Irvine, J. J., 136 n. 6, 137 n. 10, 140 n. 7
"I Won't Learn from You" and Other Thoughts on Creative Maladjustment (Kohl), 49–50, 64, 73

Jackson, A. W., 136 n. 4, 138 n. 4, 141 n. 5
Jervis, K., 136–137 n. 8
Johnson, J., 133 n. 21
Johnson, S. M., 133 n. 21, 140–141 n. 10
Junior High School 278 (Brooklyn, New York), 10–12, 14–15

Kailin, Julie, 41, 136 n. 7
Kalnin, J. S., 133–134 n. 24, 137 n. 16
Kardos, S. M., 140–141 n. 10
Katz, Michael B., 54, 138 n. 3
Katz, Susan R., 47, 137 n. 15
Kennard, B., 133–134 n. 24
King, M., 139 n. 6
Knapp, M. S., 136 n. 1
Kohl, Herbert, 18, 49–50, 56, 64, 73, 134 n. 5, 137 n. 17, 138 n. 6
Kottkamp, Robert B., 138 n. 5, 139 n. 9
Kozol, Jonathan, 18, 28, 67–68, 92, 134 n. 5, 135 n. 8, 138 n. 4, 140 n. 8, 141 n. 1
Kuzmeskus, J., 137 n. 16, 140 n. 8

Ladson-Billings, G., 136 n. 1, 136 n. 6
LaFontaine, Hernán, 12–13
Langer, J., 131–132 n. 5
Latham, A. S., 139 n. 10
Letter to Teachers, A (Perrone), 76, 96
Levin, Claudia, 139 n. 11
Levin, H., 142 n. 13
Lima, Ambrizeth H., 24–25, 39–40, 41, 51, 64, 65, 95–96, 105–106, 141 n. 10
Lipsyte, R., 142 n. 5
Lipton, M., 137 n. 13, 141 n. 6
Little, J. W., 143 n. 5
Lives on the Boundary (Rose), 50, 111
Loewen, J., 142 n. 13

Logan, Roberta, 110
Lomotey, K., 137 n. 10
Lortie, Dan C., 121, 142 n. 2
Low-track classes, 1–2
Lucas, T., 136 n. 1
Lundberg, Anne, 32–34
Lytle, Susan L., 77, 79, 133–134 n. 24, 137 n. 16, 139 n. 2, 140 n. 6, 141 n. 14, 142–143 n. 3

Macaulay, D., 142 n. 15
Magat, R., 138 n. 5
Mahiri, J., 136 n. 6
Marginalization, 5
Massachusetts Educational Reform, 65–69
Master teachers, 12
McIntyre, A., 136–137 n. 8
McKay, S. A., 132 n. 11
McLaren, P., 134 n. 3
McLaughlin, Milbrey W., 121, 131 n. 3, 142 n. 1
Meier, K. J., 132 n. 12
Melting pot myth, 25
Miller, J. L., 135 n. 12
Mindful teaching, 87–88
Moore, Henry, 115
Multicultural education
civil rights movement and, 13, 16–17, 23–24, 94
critics of, 17
importance of, 11–12
Murname, R. J., 132 n. 10

Narratives (journal), 20–21
National Center for Education Statistics, 132 n. 9, 132–133 n. 14
National Commission on Teaching and America's Future, 85, 131–132 n. 5
National Council of Teachers of English, 99
National Writing Project, 140 n. 8
Nieto, Sonia, 26–27, 28, 99, 107, 135 n. 7, 135 n. 9, 136 n. 2, 136 n. 4, 142 n. 3

Nigger (Gregory), 110
Noblitt, George W., 28–29, 135 n. 10
Noddings, Nel, 2, 132 n. 8, 133–134
    n. 24, 137 n. 9

Oakes, J., 137 n. 13, 141 n. 6
Olsen, L., 142 n. 3
Orfield, G., 133 n. 22

Parental and family involvement, 12–
    13, 14
Patchen, M., 137 n. 10
Pearson, P. D., 139–140 n. 4, 141 n. 14,
    142–143 n. 3
Pedagogy of the Oppressed (Freire), 15
Perrone, Vito, 76, 96, 142 n. 12
Poe, Edgar Allan, 87
Polinard, J. L., 132 n. 12
Politics of education, 15–16, 18–19,
    102
Pollard, D., 137 n. 10
Portes, Alejandro, 40, 136 n. 3
Poverty
    challenges of, 5–6
    education quality and, 2, 18–19, 92–
      94
Power
    culture of, 29
    of curriculum, 11–12
Preer, Anita, 54–55, 60–62, 71
Professional Communities and the
    Work of High School Teachers
    (McLaughlin and Talbert), 121
Professional development, 124–126
Project on the Next Generation of
    Teachers (Harvard University), 4
PS 25 (Bilingual School; Bronx, New
    York), 12–15
Public education
    equal education and, 92–94
    nature of school systems, 69–70
    promise of, 54–57
    urban schools, 1–3, 38–39, 92–94
Puma, M., 132 n. 11

Quartz, K. H., 137 n. 13, 141 n. 6

Racism, 4–5, 6, 17, 25, 41, 92, 94–96,
    136–137 n. 8
Raphael, Taffy, 86, 141 n. 11
Respect
    for student identity, 20–21, 39–42
    teacher indignity at lack of, 71–72
Rose, Mike, 5, 50, 111, 133–134 nn. 23–
    24, 136 n. 1, 137 n. 18, 142 n. 6
Rosenholz, S. J., 138 n. 1
Rumbaut, Rubén G., 40, 136 n. 3
Ryan, S., 132 n. 7, 137 n. 13, 141 n. 6

St. Joseph's Community School
    (Roxbury, Massachusetts), 68
Scheer, S., 135 n. 4
Schmoker, M., 143 n. 6
Schniedewind, N., 142 n. 13
Schooling in Capitalist America (Bowles
    and Gintis), 18
Schools
    climate of, 4, 9, 47
    infrastructure problems, 4
    parental and family involvement,
      12–13, 14
    racism in, 4–5, 6, 17, 25, 41, 92–96,
      136–137 n. 8
    reform of, 5, 47–49
    resegregation of, 4
    restructuring of, 5, 65–69, 126–127
School size, 108
School system, nature of, 69–70
Shea, Carol, 107
Shields, Mattie, 55, 58–59
Shields, Patrick M., 131 n. 4, 136 n. 1,
    139–140 n. 4
Shin, P. H. B., 131 n. 1
Shor, I., 134 n. 2
Silver, E. A., 142–143 n. 3
Simons, E. R., 133–134 n. 24, 137 n. 16
Sizer, N. F., 70, 139 n. 7
Sizer, Ted, 70, 94, 139 n. 7, 141 n. 8
Sleeter, C. E., 134 n. 3, 136–137 n. 8
Smith, M. S., 142–143 n. 3
Snyder, T. D., 132 n. 10
Social justice, 12–15, 91–106
    democracy and, 5, 99–105, 123

equity in education, 14–15, 18–19,
    92–94
finding equilibrium and, 105–106
poverty and, 2, 5–6, 18–19, 92–94
racism in schools and society, 4–5,
    6, 17, 25, 41, 92, 94–96, 136–137
    n. 8
struggle for equal education, 92–94
teaching as educational justice, 96–
    99
Socratic dialogue, 11
Spring, J., 134 n. 6, 138 n. 4
Standards, 2, 5, 9
Stein, M. K., 142–143 n. 3
Stinnett, T. M., 132 n. 13
Stotsky, Sandra, 134 n. 3
Student identity, teacher impact on,
    20–21, 39–42, 95–96, 119–120
Students Are Watching, The (Sizer and
    Sizer), 70
Students of color
    education quality and, 2, 3
    effective teaching and, 38–39, 132
        n. 12
    increase in numbers of, 2–3
Suzuki, Bob, 16
Sykes, G., 143 n. 5

Talbert, Joan E., 121, 131 n. 3, 142 n. 1
Teacher autobiographies, 22–36
    Judith Baker, 43–47
    Claudia Bell, 31–32, 48–49
    Patty Bode, 82–86
    Mary Cowhey, 101–105
    Sonie Felix, 56–57, 73
    Karen Gelzinis, 66–70, 112–119
    Stephen Gordon, 30–31, 79–81, 86–
        89, 97–99
    importance of, 25, 123–124
    Ambrizeth Lima, 39–40
    Anne Lundberg, 32–34
    Sonia Nieto, 26–27
    values and, 24–25, 32–33
    Junia Yearwood, 27–30, 50–51, 109–
        111
Teacher-centered education, 28–29

Teachers and teaching. See also
    Teacher autobiographies
    anger and, 63–75
    "best practices" in, 125, 128
    bilingual education and, 12–16
    caring and, 2, 29, 37–52
    challenges of, 3–6
    community and, 77–79, 90, 121–122,
        124
    compensation in, 4, 97, 128, 133 n. 19
    confidence in colleagues, 58–61
    desperation and, 72–73
    dropout/turnover, 3–4, 10, 132–133
        n. 14
    expectations for students, 20–21,
        39–43, 47, 51–52
    faith in abilities as teachers, 58
    hard work and, 10–11
    hope and, 53–62
    impact of, 20–21, 39–42, 95–96, 107–
        120
    importance of, 2, 19–21
    innovations and, 14
    intellectual work and, 76–90, 122–
        123, 126–127
    lack of respect and, 71–72
    national priorities in, 128–129
    nature of school system and, 69–70
    "passionate" teachers, 51–52, 63–64,
        128–129
    politics of education and, 15–16, 18–
        19, 102
    preparation, 15–16, 90, 107–108
    professional development and, 124–
        126
    recruitment and retention, 39
    retention problem, 3–4, 10, 132–133
        n. 14
    role in shaping futures, 107–120
    school restructuring and, 5, 65–69,
        126–127
    social justice and, 12–15, 91–106
    teachers of color, decline in
        numbers of, 2–3, 132 n. 12
    time required for, 11–12
    values and, 24–25, 32–33

Teachers as Cultural Workers (Freire), 91, 96
Tell-Tale Heart, The (Poe), 88
Treisman, P. U., 137 n. 10
Turnbull, B. J., 136 n. 1
Turning Points initiative, 94
Tutwiler, Patrick, 23, 54
Tyack, David, 94, 138 n. 4, 141 n. 5

Ullman, J., 137 n. 12
United States Bureau of the Census, 132 n. 10
University of Massachusetts, School of Education, 16–19
Urban schools
cultural and linguistic diversity in, 38–39
effective teaching in, 38–39
problems of, 1–3, 92–94

Valenzuela, A., 137 n. 9
Values, of teachers, 24–25, 32–33
Vegas, E., 132 n. 10
Viadero, D., 143 n. 7
Vygotsky, Lev, 99

Wadsworth, D., 133 n. 18
Weinberg, M., 138 n. 4

What Keeps Teachers Going in Spite of Everything? inquiry group, 6–7, 22–23, 27, 90, 127. *See also* Teacher autobiographies
What's Worth Fighting for Out There? (Hargreaves and Fullan), 70
Willett, J. B., 132 n. 10
Wilson, Suzanne M., 78, 139–140 n. 4
Wineburg, S., 140–141 n. 10
Witherell, C., 133–134 n. 24
Woolworth, S., 140–141 n. 10
Wrinkle, R. D., 132 n. 12
Writing of teachers, 79–89. See also Teacher autobiographies
call to write, 79–81
in curriculum development, 81–89
National Writing Project, 140 n. 8

Yearwood, Junia, 22–24, 25, 27–30, 29, 34–36, 37, 48, 49–51, 53, 54, 59, 63–64, 90, 108–111, 123, 128–129, 140 n. 8
Young Lords, 13
Yun, J. T., 133 n. 22

Zane, Nancie, 47, 137 n. 14
Zinn, H., 142 n. 13
Ziomek, R., 139 n. 10

ABOUT THE AUTHOR

Sonia Nieto is Professor of Language, Literacy, and Culture at the School of Education, University of Massachusetts, Amherst. She has been a teacher at all levels, from elementary through graduate school, and her research has focused on multicultural education, the education of students of culturally and linguistically diverse backgrounds, and the need for social justice in teacher education. She has written widely on these topics in such journals as the *Harvard Educational Review*, the *Journal of Teacher Education*, and *Educational Leadership*. Most notable among her books are *Affirming Diversity: The Sociopolitical Context of Multicultural Education* (Allyn & Bacon), and *The Light in Their Eyes* (Teachers College Press), both used widely in teacher education. Professor Nieto has received many awards for her research, advocacy, and activism, including the 1997 *Multicultural Educator of the Year Award* from NAME, the National Association for Multicultural Education, and a Senior Fellowship in Urban Education from the Annenberg Institute for School Reform (1998–2000). In 1999 she received an Honorary Doctorate in Humane Letters from Lesley College in Cambridge, Massachusetts, and in 2000 she was awarded a residence at the Bellagio Center in Italy.